This book is dedicated to my parents, Pat and Jack Power, who taught me the importance of taking personal responsibility for one's own financial security.

Contents

About the author

Trish Power LLB, BCom, DipArts (Professional Writing and Editing) is a financial journalist, author, and long-time share and property investor. She is also the co-founder of free superannuation website, SuperGuide <www.superguide.com.au> and free investment website, LearnerInvestor <www.learnerinvestor.com.au>.

Trish describes her financial writing as educative journalism. She also passionately believes that Australian women are entitled to clear and independent information about important issues, such as financial security and wealth creation.

Trish is interviewed regularly on radio and presents at educational investment seminars and conferences, typically speaking about superannuation, investing, property, and women and investing.

In addition to writing about super and investing, and managing her websites, Trish is endeavouring to write a novel and is always planning her next holiday. She has travelled extensively throughout Asia, the Middle East, Africa, Europe and New Zealand. Her favourite destinations are Venice, Iceland, Central Australia, Daylesford, Botswana and Petra (in Jordan).

Acknowledgements

A huge thanks to my test readers for reviewing an advanced draft of *Super Freedom* and providing such valuable feedback. In alphabetical order, these wonderful and generous women are:

- Kim Clifford

- Sally Haines

- Renee Ludekens

- Siobhan McHale

- Julianne Power

- Maree Power

- Irene Salmont.

Robert Drake from the Australian Securities and Investments Commission was always available to answer my emails regarding the ASIC MoneySmart calculators. Many thanks, Robert, for your assistance.

Also, a special thanks to acquisitions editor Kristen Hammond for believing in the possibility of this book and her ongoing counsel. A big thank you to the rest of the dedicated Wiley team for their contribution to the production of this book, including Clare Weber, Dani Karvess, Meryl Potter (my talented editor) and Elizabeth Whiley.

Introduction:
Financial freedom is possible

> *We are constantly being told that we've never been wealthier.*
> *And many of us are. On average we all are.*
> *But that's just the problem ... no one is average.*

Julia Gillard, first female Prime Minister of Australia

I have wanted to write this book for a long time because it seems that many women believe that financial freedom, particularly in retirement, is not possible. A financially stress-free retirement is indeed possible, and the easiest way to achieve this dream is by getting to know how the superannuation (super) rules can benefit you.

This book can help you discover how you can create a better life for yourself financially in six steps, and you don't have to spend thousands of dollars in financial advice to make this happen.

If there is a single message I hope all readers will take from this book, it would be: it is never too late, or too early, to improve your financial circumstances.

It's about the life you want in retirement

I have spoken at many seminars where women in the audience would approach me after the presentation and say, for example: 'Now I understand what my superannuation savings can create for me — why didn't someone tell me this earlier?' Other women would comment on the fact that I talked their language, rather than the language of the money men.

Many readers of my consumer website, SuperGuide at <www.superguide. com.au>, were pleasantly surprised that they now had information they could understand that could improve their lives. For example, one female reader wrote: 'I don't feel so overwhelmed any more now that I have a source where it is easy to find information'.

It was fantastic to receive such lovely feedback from seminar participants, and from readers of my website, but I also appreciated that there is a real problem. Although the superannuation industry is spending millions of dollars to encourage Australians to think about planning for retirement, many women are not hearing the message. Although the government is offering tax incentives to save for retirement by using a superannuation fund, many women are not taking advantage of these incentives. Why not?

I have worked in, or written about, the superannuation industry for nearly 25 years, and the answer to this question is patently clear to me. Many women haven't been heeding the plan for retirement message because most of the information available about superannuation and retirement is not targeted towards women; rather, it is targeted towards some average person that rarely resembles a female.

Women have different life experiences from men

The first question I was asked when I told some female friends that I was writing a book for women on superannuation and retirement was: 'Why does there need to be a book on super especially for women? Don't men have to think about this stuff too?'

Yes, men do have to think about this stuff, but women have to deal with this stuff in a different way from men.

A male friend of mine suggested I should just add a supplement chapter to one of my existing books, explaining the special issues women face when planning for retirement. On the surface, his suggestion had merit because my existing books were certainly written with both female and male readers in mind, but as you probably already know, there are bigger issues playing out for women wanting to create a better life for themselves in retirement.

Although we may all like to think women and men are the same in terms of money and finance, women generally have different life experiences from men, such as:

- earning less (on average)

- living longer than men (on average), which generally means women need to save more for retirement than men, or live a more modest life in retirement

- taking time out of the workforce to bring up children

- continuing to be the main carer of children from a marriage or other type of previous relationship in the event of divorce or separation

- reducing or rescheduling work hours to care for an elderly parent or parents

- for most women in their fifties or older, not being given the option of having a super account until much later in life, if at all.

The major difference between a man and woman, when saving for retirement, is directly linked to the fact that the most popular way of saving for retirement is through Australia's superannuation (super) system. The Australian super system was originally designed for a traditional male who worked full time for 35 years and remained married to the one person for his entire life. If you don't fit into the traditional male definition—and most women (and some men) don't—then you definitely need to be more hands-on with your retirement planning.

Women learn differently from men on money matters

The superannuation system has certainly improved over the years, although women who don't work full time, or women who are self-employed, definitely have to think more creatively when it comes to saving and planning for retirement. What's new? I believe thinking outside the box has always been a necessity for women, and this can reap unexpected financial rewards. For instance, you may be surprised by the fact that a study has shown that women are better investors than men. I will share some of the findings from this fascinating study in chapter 2.

In addition, in terms of finance and money, women often learn differently from men. Women like to discover the benefits of a product or service, or what it can deliver for them. Men like to do that too but many men also love to get under the hood and see how something works.

In my experience, the process of how superannuation works seems to engage the blokes more than the women, and for some crazy reason the main focus in Australia seems to be on the process of saving for your retirement—typically the superannuation rules. I believe the focus should be more on the outcome—wanting a comfortable life in retirement.

Clearly the super rules are essential information, but such information is most helpful when you know what lifestyle you want in retirement, and how much money is necessary — your retirement target — to deliver that lifestyle. You can then use the superannuation rules to help you reach your retirement target.

In other words, much of the information available on retirement planning explains what the super rules are, rather than explaining how you can create the retirement lifestyle that you want by using the super rules. This book is different, and the information is tailored to the life experiences of women.

Women often have to work smarter, think smarter and tailor a standard system to suit their unique needs. Fortunately, women are highly adept at doing this because most women, in most parts of their life, are facing similar issues, whether it be raising children, managing work–life balance, tackling the boys' club in society or traditionally male workplaces, or working in undervalued female-dominated industries.

The aim of my book is to help you work out the steps necessary to create a worry-free lifestyle in retirement, and superannuation just happens to be one of the easiest ways to get there.

Every woman deserves the opportunity to discover her own retirement dream, and this book gives you some handy tools to help make that dream come true. I hope you enjoy *Super Freedom*.

Trish Power

Part 1

It's never too late or too early to create a super future

Unlocking the super secrets to a wealthy life

> When women thrive, all of society benefits, and succeeding
> generations are given a better start in life.
>
> *Kofi Annan, former secretary-general of the United Nations,*
> *and co-recipient of the 2001 Nobel Peace Prize*

I dislike the word superannuation, because it seems to stop many women from getting excited about a creating a great life for themselves in retirement. Let's ignore the word for a moment, and think about how you want to live in retirement. How do you picture your life when you finish working?

I'll give you my dream for my retirement. In no particular order, I want to be able to hang out in cafés regularly, pursue any interest or hobby that takes my fancy, spend time with family and friends, travel reasonably regularly, take long walks at any time of the day, read books, write a novel or two, continue to help Australians create better lives for themselves, *and* I don't want to worry about whether I can pay my bills or afford to go out for dinner. I also want to have reasonable health, which means I need to factor in regular exercise.

Now, that's my retirement dream, and that's what I consider to be a very wealthy life. Your dream of a wealthy retirement is likely to be different from mine.

Wealth is in the eye of the beholder

Some fantastic retirement plans that I have heard include:

- I don't want to have to stress about paying bills, or have sleepless nights over the cost of maintaining the house, or worry about whether I can afford to buy gifts for my children or grandchildren.

- I want to have my mortgage paid off.

- I don't want to be renting when I'm retired.

- I want to travel overseas once a year, and be able to afford to run a holiday house for our extended family.

- I want to buy a caravan and travel around Australia for a year, and then return home and travel once a year for two months.

- I want to build the most beautiful garden I can possibly create, and then have open garden days for charity.

- I want to go out for dinner any night of the week we choose, have a cleaner and help our children buy houses.

- I want to run a bed and breakfast in the country for 10 years, and then convert the cottage into our home.

- I just want to be free of drudgery and constant financial sacrifice.

- I want to be able to give back to the community, without having to worry about my own financial security.

What's your dream for your life in retirement? Have a think about it. Whatever your dream turns out to be, the common theme that runs through all dreams for retirement is *how* to get there. The encouraging news is that it is easier than most people expect.

By applying the tools contained in this book, I know roughly how much my own retirement dream will cost me. Without much change to my current lifestyle, I've already put the steps in place to ensure that I can live the life I want when I'm no longer working. I no longer worry about retirement (another intimidating word) because I have taken my own advice and conducted my Six-Step Wealth Check.

The tools described in this book may help you too. You can do your own Six-Step Wealth Check, for free, using this book as your guide.

Obviously, retirement is not just a money thing. Financial security is extremely important for a happy retirement but let's put our retirement plans in perspective. Every week, I meet retirees living solely on the Age Pension (the government-funded aged-based pension) who live a happy life because they maintain family and community relationships, look after their health and make sure they have fun. Now their definition of fun may not be your definition of fun, but my point is that wealth can have many meanings.

It's never too late to start, or too early to think about it

You may be single, divorced with kids, married, living with someone, widowed or gay — this book has you in mind. You may be age 25, 35, 45, 55 or older, and want greater financial freedom — this book has you in mind.

If you are reading this chapter, then you've already overcome the second most difficult part of retirement planning — thinking about it! I can already hear the question — if that's the second most difficult aspect, what is the most difficult?

The most difficult aspect of creating a financially secure life for yourself when you retire is — getting started. Okay, getting started is really not that difficult but most of us have mastered the art of procrastination and taking the first steps can often be challenging.

If the prospect of changing your financial future is daunting, and you're looking for instant inspiration and motivation, then you may want to head directly to what I believe are the most exciting chapters in the book:

- Chapter 4: Your Six-Step Wealth Check: how much money is enough?

- Chapter 5: Case study — I'm 52. Is it too late to start saving?

- Chapter 7: Doing a little: turn $4500 into $300000 the easy way

- Chapter 8: Doing a lot: making $1 million is possible, but it takes a super plan

- Chapter 9: Case studies — four women create $1 million nest eggs

I have structured the book in a way that enables you to dream for a while and look at possibilities before having to embark on any first steps.

If you're looking for reasons *not* to take control of your super future, then I suggest you check out chapter 2. I have spoken with thousands of women over the years and I have heard nearly as many reasons why they believe they can't take control of their financial future. In chapter 2, I have the answers for the top 14 monkeys on your back — the reasons, or excuses, we all use for not getting started with our retirement planning.

In most cases, the real reasons for not getting started are temporary, or relate to confidence or the lack of relevant information.

And when you're ready to get serious about your retirement planning, I offer you 15 tips that can help you grow your wealth through superannuation (see chapter 10). The first five tips are quickies that you can do during a lazy afternoon, and the next five tips can help you really change your life with minimal cost, while the final five tips can help set you up for a financially stress-free retirement.

I also take you for a trip into the future to see what your retirement in financial terms is going to look like, including how much Age Pension you can expect to receive, and what happens to your superannuation benefits when you embark on your life of leisure. (Throughout the book, I use capital letters when referring to the government-funded Age Pension, to differentiate from a superannuation pension or income stream that you may receive from your super fund.)

The entire book deals with all types of women, although I do want to make an important point about women who may be single or divorced or widowed. Most women at some stage in their lives will live alone — either by choice or by circumstance. You may never marry; you may be single before you marry; you may divorce; you may outlive your husband or partner; or you may end up living apart because your partner (or you) suffers aged-related illness. Many wealth accumulation books don't cater for women living on their own, but my book certainly does.

Okay, what's so great about boring superannuation?

In the past, when I have mentioned to women that I write about superannuation I often received one of two responses: the less tactful responded with 'boring' or, more precisely, 'boooorrrrinnnng!'; a typical alternative response was: 'Super! I hardly have any of that', and then a quick change of subject. I don't blame them really, because as I explain in the introduction to this book, much of the information available about planning for retirement doesn't seem to have women in mind.

A super means to an exciting end

When I do encounter this type of response I usually expand on what I write about by explaining that I show people how to create better lives for themselves using six easy steps. The response is then very different: for example, some may say 'Really?' (and I mean a genuine, rather polite 'Really?') or say, 'Oh, so what are the six steps?'

It seems that many of those women who find superannuation boring also love to discuss what they want to do when they don't have to work so hard, or when the kids have grown up or when they simply don't have to work any more. The most rewarding part of the conversation is when the penny drops, and these women realise what superannuation is all about—it is simply a means to a hopefully happy and financially stress-free retirement.

Superannuation is not the only way to create a better life in retirement, but it's without doubt one of the easiest ways to get there. If you work regularly, your employer must contribute money to your super account. The contributions in your super account are invested on your behalf, and the investment earnings on those contributions are reinvested regularly. While you're going about your daily life, your super savings are growing over time.

You can also add your own money to your super account—leading to more savings and more earnings.

Even if you choose not to take an interest in your super, your super account is still accumulating wealth on your behalf. If you choose to take more control over your superannuation savings you can help create the lifestyle you want for your retirement.

Reap the benefits of a tax-friendly savings scheme

The Australian government rewards you with incentives if you save for your retirement using a superannuation account. The general deal is that you must keep your super benefits in your super fund until you retire, and in return your super account pays a maximum tax rate of 15 per cent on fund earnings. For many Australians, 15 per cent tax is lower than the tax rate they can expect to pay on their personal income and non-superannuation investment earnings (see appendix for income tax rates).

You may also be able to reduce your income tax bill by making voluntary concessional super contributions, depending on your level of income. A concessional contribution is a super contribution that an employer, or you, claims a tax deduction for, or that reduces your taxable salary. When the contribution enters your super fund, 15 per cent tax is deducted from the contribution amount. If you're employed, your employer's compulsory super contributions (required to be made by your employer under the superannuation guarantee laws) are treated as concessional contributions, and so are your voluntary salary sacrifice contributions (if any)—I explain the different types of super contributions and what they can do for your retirement savings in chapter 6.

You can also expect tax-free super benefits when you retire. When you retire on or after the age of 60, you receive your superannuation benefits free of income tax, unless you were a long-term public servant (and then you may pay a little bit of tax—see chapter 11 for more information).

It's about looking long term

Apart from the unique tax advantages associated with superannuation, your super account and the investments that your super fund makes on your behalf, operate like any other long-term investment. Your superannuation account can help you accumulate wealth in the following ways:

- If you're an employee, your employer makes compulsory super contributions to your super. The compulsory employer contributions are officially known as superannuation guarantee (SG) contributions.

- You can add to your super savings by making voluntary super contributions, which can take the form of concessional (before-tax) or non-concessional (after-tax) contributions.

- Your super fund invests in a variety of assets, such as shares and property, that generally increase in value over time, but can sometimes drop in value too.

- Any investment earnings that your super account receives are reinvested to buy more investments, creating further earnings on top of existing earnings. This concept is known as compound earnings, which can dramatically increase your capacity to accumulate wealth.

Having a superannuation account may be your first experience with investments. This book includes an introduction to investing (see chapter 3) for readers who are interested in finding out more about how investing works, and how sensible investing can be your doorway to a financially stress-free retirement. Even if you already appreciate the importance of maintaining the purchasing power of your money through investment, you may still find chapter 3 a helpful refresher. Don't go there just yet: we have some monkey business to discuss in chapter 2 first.

Good news alert no. 1: don't forget the Age Pension

Before you head off to the next chapter, remember that your superannuation account may not be your only source of savings in retirement, and you may already be in a better financial position than you realise. You might have other investments or savings, or you may receive an inheritance at some stage.

Also, most retirees receive at least a part Age Pension even when they have substantial savings, and around half of all retirees receive a full Age Pension (see chapter 11).

Getting the monkeys off your back: what's stopping you from taking super control?

> 66 You can avoid reality, but you cannot avoid the consequences 99
> of avoiding reality.

Ayn Rand, author and philosopher

For so many women, the needs of other people usually come first — children, partner, parents, friends and even workmates. Often, for a woman to think about her own needs, she has to face a health challenge, financial stress or a relationship breakdown.

Too dramatic, perhaps? I don't think so. The world that women live in is slowly changing, but most women have been raised to think of others before themselves. If we think of our own needs, we may even be considered selfish, by others or even ourselves.

Thinking of others is an admirable quality, but it's possible to look after your own needs and still do great things for others. Sometimes, it can take an entire lifetime before a woman discovers that the best way to look after other people is to look after herself as well.

I can almost hear you say: 'Hey, I thought this was a wealth accumulation book, not a self-help book'. For those who may be holding the view that wealth accumulation is just about money, I ask the following question: until now, what's stopped you from thinking about saving for your retirement?

Naming the top 14 monkeys holding back super plans

From my conversations with thousands of women over the years, I have compiled a list of the top 14 monkeys that seem to sit on the backs of many women, and stop them from taking super control.

1 Superannuation is boring, and I'm only reading this book because a girlfriend gave it to me as a gift.

2 I don't know enough about investing and super.

3 I only have $15 000 in super. What's the point?

4 I can't afford to buy a house; retirement is the least of my worries.

5 Paying off my house is more important than putting money into super.

6 I'm not working, so how can I possibly think about saving for retirement?

7 I'm too busy with my kids to think about super and investing.

8 We have a mortgage and we are paying school fees — we have no spare cash to put into super.

9 I'm divorced and raising children — I don't think I'll ever be able to retire.

10 I'm in my fifties, and now it's too late.

11 My husband/partner is my retirement plan.

12 My husband/partner looks after all of our finances.

13 I have super but I don't know where it is.

14 I'm self-employed and superannuation is not a priority.

I applied some creativity to the first monkey but the remaining monkeys are compiled from real-life conversations with Australian women.

Monkey 1: Superannuation is boring, and I'm only reading this book because a girlfriend gave it to me as a gift

Advice is what we ask for when we already know the answer but wish we didn't.

Erica Jong, author and feminist

Well, you have a very good friend who must have excellent judgement, since she made the decision to buy this special book for you. Seriously, your friend must care for you very much if she took the risk to buy you a money book as a gift, when you think superannuation is boring. Your friend is either very worried about your financial security in retirement, or my book has helped your friend with her own plans for retirement. In either case, your friend's gift is probably a sign you should keep on reading. You may be pleasantly surprised by what you discover.

Monkey 2: I don't know enough about investing and super

That is what learning is. You suddenly understand something you've understood all your life, but in a new way.

Doris Lessing, *author and political activist*

Lack of confidence about superannuation and investment matters is a common issue for many Australians, including many women. Fortunately, you have picked an ideal super book to start your journey. In this book, I assume most readers are not experienced in investing or know little about super. But, as you read through the book, you're likely to discover that you know more than you realise.

And the very best news is this: on average, women are better investors than men. According to a study conducted in the United States by Merrill Lynch Investment Managers, women make fewer mistakes when investing than men, and when women do make a mistake, they are less likely than men to make the same mistake again.

Okay, according to the study, men are more knowledgeable than women about investing, but that doesn't make them better investors. The difference with female investors is that, on average, women know what they don't know about investing and aren't afraid to ask experts for assistance, while men are more likely to make investment decisions on the basis of greed, overconfidence or impatience.

The key message to take from the US study is that the naturally cautious approach many women use when investing can lead to investment success over time.

Monkey 3: I only have $15 000 in super. What's the point?

Optimism is the faith that leads to achievement. Nothing can be done without hope or confidence.

Helen Keller, author, suffragist and pacifist

You have a very popular monkey on your back. I have heard this type of comment, and many similar comments, nearly every time the topic of superannuation and retirement comes up in a conversation.

So, what's the point in saving for retirement? That's the wrong question to ask. What you are really asking is: how on earth can $15 000 help me in retirement?

Retiring today with $15 000

If you retire today and you have **$15 000** in super savings then you can expect to have a retirement income of nearly **$20 000** a year (as a single woman) or just under **$30 000** a year (as a couple) when you include your full Age Pension entitlements. Surprised?

The deal in Australia is that in retirement most Australians receive a full or part Age Pension in addition to any income they may receive from their super savings and non-super savings. You can receive around $19 000 a year (as a single person) and you can still have just over $180 000 in savings and assets, plus your home. As a couple, you can receive around $29 000 in Age Pension entitlements, and own around $260 000 in savings and assets, plus your home.

Using the free retirement planner calculator on the Australian Securities and Investments Commission (ASIC) MoneySmart website, the $15 000 in super savings can deliver roughly $900 a year in income until an individual reaches the age of 87, which can supplement your Age Pension entitlement.

Imagine what a few extra thousand dollars can do to your lifestyle in retirement if you started to do some planning.

> **Tip**
>
> In addition to six-monthly adjustments to the Age Pension rates, from July 2012, a person's Age Pension entitlement will include a clean energy supplement (subject to the legislation being passed). This means that when the Age Pension adjustments take effect, the annual retirement incomes quoted under Monkey 3 will increase by a few hundred dollars (see chapter 11 for more information).

Retiring later, and employer super contributions

If you start off with **$15 000** in super and your employer continues to contribute to your super account over your working life, then by just turning up for work, your $15 000 can potentially deliver you hundreds of thousands of dollars. For example, by turning up for work for 30 years while earning $50 000 a year, you can turn $15 000 into nearly **$500 000** in tomorrow's dollars, which translates into just over **$260 000** in today's dollars.

> **Tip**
>
> Talking about today's dollars helps you compare what the future amount could buy you if you retired with the equivalent amount today (see chapter 3 for more information).

For a single person, a retirement balance of **$260 000** in today's dollars can translate into a retirement income of just over **$33 000** a year in today's dollars (including a substantial part Age Pension) until the age of 87, or just over **$30 000** a year (including substantial part Age Pension) until the age of 100.

For a couple, a retirement balance of **$260 000** can translate into a retirement income of nearly **$45 000** until the age of 87 (including nearly a full Age Pension), or just over **$41 000** until the age of 100 (including nearly a full Age Pension), based on the figures produced by the ASIC MoneySmart retirement planner calculator.

If you ask the right questions, starting with a $15 000 account balance in your super fund can change your life. Even when you currently have no super, you can change your life by finding the answers to the right questions, and then taking super control.

> ## Tip
>
> Throughout the book, I use freely available online calculators when quoting figures in case studies and other text. You can apply your own level of income and your own super balance to work out what you can expect to receive in retirement. I explain the assumptions behind the Monkey 3 calculations in the appendix.

Monkey 4: I can't afford to buy a house; retirement is the least of my worries

The minute you settle for less than you deserve, you get even less than you settled for.

Maureen Dowd, author and columnist

You're actually carrying two monkeys. If you have this load on your back, then you're probably feeling unmotivated, considering that you have all that weight pushing you down.

We need to deal with each of your monkeys in turn. Owning your own place is a big deal, particularly in Australia where the availability of public housing for lower income earners is dismal. The issue of housing affordability is really another book, but what we *plan* to live in when we work and retire is often very different from what we *need* to live in when we work and retire. Having aspirations of what a first home (or home in retirement) should be is fine, but a first home or apartment is rarely the dream home. Often, purchasing a first home involves huge compromises on your initial expectations.

You may actively choose to rent rather than buy a home, or you may have no choice but to rent for a significant period of your life. Financial circumstances can change over time, but if you do intend to rent in retirement, then planning for your retirement becomes even more important because you have to factor in the cost of rent.

The other monkey that you're carrying—'retirement is the least of my worries'—is a universal monkey for many Australian women. For example, variations of monkey 4 include:

- I have just started work; retirement is the least of my worries

- I have just bought a house … (see monkey 5)

- We have just had kids … (see monkey 7)

- We are paying the mortgage and school fees … (see monkey 8)

So, what you seem to be saying is that because you don't own your home, you're not going to try to improve the life you can have when you retire. Well, if you're planning to rent when you retire, then I believe you have even more incentive to plan for your retirement. For example, you will need to allow for periodic rental increases during retirement. You may also face the possibility of being forced to move during your retirement, if the rental property you are living in is sold.

You will be surprised how easy it is to change your financial circumstances for retirement. Even a small level of savings can dramatically improve your standard of living compared with living solely on the Age Pension.

> ## Tip
>
> If you're single and you plan to rent when you retire, then I urge you to start thinking about your retirement now, and what you want it to look like. Single women relying solely on the Age Pension, who also rent, usually financially struggle most in retirement (see chapter 11 for more information on Age Pension entitlements). The Australian government is slowly trying to redress the issue of affordable housing for Australians, but it is never a good idea to leave your financial future to the political whims of future governments.

Monkey 5: Paying off my house is more important than putting money into super

Not everything that can be counted counts, and not everything that counts can be counted.

Albert Einstein, physicist, philosopher and world-famous genius

Many women relate to this monkey, and some may question whether it is a monkey at all. Paying off a home loan improves your financial security for retirement, so is it really a problem whether someone focuses on repaying the home loan, or instead focuses on making super contributions?

The answer is no: it isn't a problem if someone decides to focus on repaying the mortgage because the financial choices you make depend on your personal circumstances. The issue is not whether someone makes a decision to repay a mortgage rather than adding extra money to a super account. The issue is whether such a decision is always an either/or decision.

In most cases, if you can afford to pay off a mortgage it means you're also working. Even if you can't make extra contributions, or you choose not to make extra contributions, your employer will still be contributing to your superannuation account.

Monkey 6: I'm not working, so how can I possibly think about saving for retirement?

The key to realising a dream is to focus not on success but on significance – and then even the small steps and little victories along your path will take on greater meaning.

Oprah Winfrey, TV personality, billionaire and philanthropist

In everyone's life, there will be times when it is not possible to make extra contributions to a superannuation account because today's financial concerns are more pressing. Even if you're not working, your existing super benefits are accumulating while you're getting on with life.

You may not be working now, but for most women, time out of the workforce is generally not a permanent condition. For example, many women who have children eventually return to full-time or part-time work.

The time when you're not working is probably a perfect opportunity to start thinking about the life that you want in retirement. True, you probably can't afford to put money into super, or save money, but you can certainly do some planning. It's also an excellent time to do a financial stocktake, that is, work out what superannuation and savings you currently have.

If you're in a relationship and not working, then you're also in an ideal position to plan for the future, on behalf of your partner and yourself. Time can be an extremely valuable resource when you are planning for retirement.

Monkey 7: I'm too busy with my kids to think about super and investing

Always be nice to your children because they are the ones who will choose your rest home.

Phyllis Diller, comedian

Sometimes the life of today is a higher priority than the life of tomorrow, but tomorrow will eventually arrive.

If you decide the right time for planning for retirement is later down the track, you can still help your retirement plans along with minimal effort. Here are four things that you can do:

- Continue reading this book.
- Find out how much money is enough for the life that you want in retirement (I take you through this process later in the book).
- Try my Six-Step Wealth Check (see chapter 4).
- Take note of at least the first five tips on how to boost your super savings in chapter 10. You could save thousands of dollars.

And remember, your kids will grow up and face similar issues to you when planning for their retirement. Wouldn't it be great if you could guide them through this important phase later in life as well?

Monkey 8: We have a mortgage and we are paying school fees—we have no spare cash to put into super

Success is getting what you want; happiness is wanting what you get.

Ingrid Bergman, actress

You're not alone. As is the case with monkey 7 (too busy with kids), sometimes the current financial pressures of life take greater priority. Even when home loans and children are the main focus, consider the following comments:

- Your existing super accounts are still working for you.

- If you're working (including part time), your employer continues to contribute to your super account.

- Now is the perfect time to do a spot of retirement planning. Reading this book is a great start!

Monkey 9: I'm divorced and raising children—I don't think I'll ever be able to retire

Being defeated is often a temporary condition. Giving up is what makes it permanent.

Marilyn vos Savant, author and columnist

Raising children on your own can be challenging enough without the worry of how you're going to finance your life in retirement after your children have grown up.

If you're a full-time carer of children and not in paid employment, then your options to take immediate action on your retirement plans may have to be delayed for a while. Even so, there are numerous things you can do now that can help your life in retirement, including:

- You probably can't put money into super, or save money, but you may be able to do some planning for the future.

- Planning for the future can be as simple as reading this book.

- Check out the case studies later in the book for ideas on how to improve your retirement lifestyle after you have taken time out of the workforce to raise your children.

- Take note of the free tips that can save you thousands of dollars scattered throughout the book (especially the first five tips in chapter 10).

If you're working part time, or full time, then your employer is contributing money towards your retirement, even if you don't have the cash, time or energy to currently devote to your retirement plans.

Monkey 10: I'm in my fifties, and now it's too late

You gain strength, courage and confidence by every experience in which you really stop to look fear in the face. You must do the thing which you think you cannot do.

Eleanor Roosevelt, political activist and former first lady of the United States

It's never too late to save for your retirement, and I have a case study to demonstrate to you what's possible. The case study tells Irene's story. Irene is 52 years of age and earns an annual income of **$39 000**. She is worried that she has left it too late to create a better life for herself in retirement. Not so! If she contributes **$100** a week to her super fund, Irene can have a similar lifestyle in retirement to the one that she is enjoying now. Read about Irene's story in chapter 5.

Monkey 11: My husband/partner is my retirement plan

It is a truth universally acknowledged, that a single man in possession of a good fortune, must be in want of a wife.

Jane Austen, early 19th century author

The idea that a woman relies on her husband or partner for financial security may sound old-fashioned, but the reality is that if you have children, it's likely that the partner who hasn't borne the child is the main bread-winner.

Due to taking time out of the workforce to raise children, your income-earning potential can be affected when you eventually return to work and, crude though it sounds, for many women, the deal has been struck that the couple will rely mainly on the husband's or partner's superannuation and other savings. Such an arrangement may make perfect sense for the couple involved unless one of the following events occur:

- the couple divorce (visit my free website SuperGuide at <www.superguide.com.au> for information on super rights in the event of a divorce)

- the income-earning partner dies or suffers serious illness (visit my free website SuperGuide for information about the importance of life insurance and disability insurance)

- the income-earning partner faces redundancy from employment

- your partner is useless with money.

In most relationships, usually one partner deals with the financial affairs. But you can never be complacent about retirement plans that rely on the behaviour of someone other than yourself, even if that other person is your lifelong partner. I hold strong views that, even where you don't deal with the detail of your financial affairs, you should be fully aware of the health, or otherwise, of your savings and investments and the implications for you and your family if hardship or tragedy strikes.

Monkey 12: My husband/partner looks after all of our finances

The first problem for all of us, men and women, is not to learn, but to unlearn.

Gloria Steinem, feminist and political activist

Since the traditional 1950s, the world has changed a lot, but if you're over the age of 50 you were probably part of what I call the princess generation—your mother, or father, instilled in you that the deal was to get married (to a handsome prince) and then your husband would look after you, and look after the finances.

It wasn't that long ago that a woman couldn't get a bank loan or start a business without a man, or be taken seriously unless a man was supporting her point of view. For example, I have a friend in her early forties who was denied a bank loan in her twenties because she might get pregnant.

If you have children and you have stopped work for a while, you may have passed financial control over to your spouse because he is earning the income (see monkey 11).

In many relationships, the usual practice is to divide up the responsibilities of the household for convenience, or to suit each partner's strengths. Many women are the money managers in households in terms of budgeting and household bills, but from my many chats with women, many more men than women look after the family investments (if any), although this traditional split of roles has been slowly changing in recent times.

If you're not involved in your family's finances or investments, I suggest you ask your partner the following questions:

1   What are the names of our super funds?

2   How much money do we have in each of our superannuation accounts?

3   How much super does my employer and your employer contribute each year?

4   How much credit card debt do we have?

5   Do we have any outstanding household bills?

6   How much do we owe on our home loan, and other loans?

7   How is our retirement plan going?

If your partner cannot answer all of these questions, then I suggest you take a greater interest in your finances and your future financial security. This book will help you answer questions 1, 2, 3 and 7 from the list above.

Monkey 13: I have super but I don't know where it is

It is what we make of what we have, not what we are given, that separates one person from another.

Nelson Mandela, former President of South Africa, human rights activist

This is one of the easiest monkeys to lift from your back. If you can remember where you have worked, you should be able to find your superannuation accounts. If you can't recall your work history, then you still have a good chance of finding your lost super if you know your tax file number.

Each year, your superannuation fund sends you a member statement reporting your account balance and your fund's investment returns. If you're not receiving these statements, then you will need to hunt down your superannuation statements from your superannuation fund, or super funds (if you belong to more than one fund).

If you don't know which super fund you belong to, that's okay too, because special services are available to help you find your lost super accounts. You could become thousands of dollars richer simply by making a phone call, or visiting a website (see tip 2 on p. 153 for more information on how to find your lost super accounts).

Monkey 14: I'm self-employed and superannuation is not a priority

Retirement is wonderful if you have two essentials – much to live on and much to live for.

Anonymous

Under the superannuation laws, if you're self-employed you're not required to set aside money to contribute to a super fund. The only exception is where a self-employed individual has structured her business as a company and then she (her company) must pay SG (compulsory employer super contributions) to eligible employees (including herself). (See chapter 6 for an explanation of the SG laws.)

If you're self-employed, your retirement plans, and whether you do anything about those plans, are left totally up to you. For many Australians who run businesses the easy decision is to focus on growing the business, rather than dedicating valuable cash to any long-term retirement plans.

If you're building value in your business over time, then opting for such a strategy (leaving saving for retirement to a later stage) may be the way to go, because the superannuation laws do recognise that for many business owners, the business itself forms an important part of a business owner's retirement plan, and the tax laws provide some generous incentives when a business is sold.

If, however, as a self-employed person your time, labour and expertise are the key value of the business, then you need to ask yourself whether you will have a business to sell when you retire. If you *are* the business, then you can't rely on the sale of your business to finance your retirement because you may have nothing to sell when you leave the business. If you are in this position, then your retirement planning starts now.

As a self-employed individual you can make tax-deductible super contributions and non-concessional (after-tax) super contributions. You can also take advantage of the co-contribution scheme, if your income is below a certain level. If you're able to sell your business, then you may also have access to the small business retirement exemption and other retirement-related incentives. (See chapter 6 for an explanation of the contribution rules that apply to self-employed individuals, and also see my free website SuperGuide at <www.superguide.com.au> for more detail on super, the self-employed and small business.)

Chapter 3

Investing for super beginners

Once upon a time there was a young woman named Jane. She had never heard the word superannuation before so she asked her mum what the word meant. Her mum told her that superannuation is when money is put aside, like deferring some of your pay, for a better lifestyle later on in life. Her mum said if you have a job you can expect your employer to pay money to a special account run by a superannuation fund. You can even make your own deposits into the superannuation account if you want more money for your life later on.

Jane went away and thought about this thing called superannuation, and wondered what would happen to her own superannuation for the next 20 or 30 years, until she needed it later on in her life. She asked her mum. Her mother released a deep sigh, realising the importance of this moment, and put the kettle on. She told her daughter to take a seat and promised to start from the very beginning. And so she began the story of how a superannuation account was created, and how the money in Jane's super account was transformed into investments...

Okay, the brief story above is the beginning of an unrealistic fairy tale, but in an ideal world, we would be taught about finances, investing and superannuation by our parents or by schools, like we're taught about reading, writing, manners, the facts of life and possibly even the merits of common sense. The reality is that most of us were never given the opportunity to learn about investing. If you're lucky enough to know a lot about investing then you either had parents who were investors, or you taught yourself about investing.

Although this book is not strictly an investment book, a superannuation fund invests money on behalf of its members, which means how you and your super fund invest is an important contributor to your retirement wealth.

This chapter fills in some of the gaps for those women who have never been exposed to investing, and provides a refresher for those who have forgotten the difference between saving and investing, or forgotten the importance of maintaining the purchasing power of their hard-earned money.

You can read this chapter in one sitting, or treat it as a reference to dip in and out of while reading the rest of the book. If you are an experienced investor, then you could scan this chapter and move on to chapter 4, or you can linger over the fascinating examples illustrating the delights of compound earnings. Go on, be tempted.

For a more detailed resource on investing, I suggest you check out my book, *You Don't Have to Be Rich to Become Wealthy: The Baby Boomers Investment Bible* (Wrightbooks, 2007), which was co-authored with Ian Murdoch and Jamie Nemtsas. Despite the book title, you don't have to be a baby boomer to benefit from the book.

Drumroll—the key elements of wealth generation

If you scan the financial pages of any newspaper you're likely to find advertisements promoting money-making schemes. Many of these schemes require you to undertake expensive courses and often involve high-risk strategies.

Unless you're planning to be a full-time professional investor who buys and sells investments regularly, the basic principles of investing and creating wealth are not complex. The key elements to accumulating wealth, consistently over time, are:

- Don't spend more than you earn, unless you are borrowing to invest in quality assets.

- Have some type of plan—it doesn't have to be a formal plan, but you need to have some idea of what you want in the end, and the risks you're willing to take to get there.

- Invest wisely—understand what you invest in, or what your super fund invests in, and if you're worried about the possibility of losing money, ensure you spread your savings over different asset classes and different investments.

• Don't spend your investment earnings, yet! Instead, reinvest your investment earnings and enjoy the benefits of compound earnings.

Saving money is different from investing

Investing means making your money work as hard as you do. Investing also means your money is working for you even when you're sleeping, or on holidays, or taking time out of the workforce to raise children or to return to study.

The most enticing feature of investing your money (and having your money in a superannuation account means your money is usually being invested by investment experts) is that you have your money working *for you*, rather than *you* working *for your money*.

The concept of saving as opposed to investing can often be confusing. For example, if you have your money in a bank account that pays no interest, then that bank account is not an investment. You may have savings but those savings are not working for you, as an investment would. If, however, the bank pays interest on your bank account balance, then your account can be considered an investment, because the bank account is generating a return in the form of interest. Depending on what level of interest (the return) the bank pays on your account, you may consider it's a good investment or bad investment.

Compound earnings make you richer

The easiest way to accumulate wealth in a steady fashion is by reinvesting the earnings from your investments. You then earn more interest (or investment earnings) on your interest, which means your investments grow faster over time.

One of the key advantages of superannuation is also seen as one of its key disadvantages. Many people complain that they can't access their superannuation until they retire, but this rule also means that your super account's investment earnings are reinvested regularly for a long time. Keeping your investment earnings in your super fund for 10, 20 or 30 years, or even longer, means you're building a much bigger nest egg for your retirement than you could have achieved if you were able to withdraw your money at any time.

Doubling your money is all about time

Want to double your money? Depending on the risk that you're willing to take, you can double a one-off investment in four to five years—though it's more likely that it will take between seven and 10 years, assuming you re-invest your earnings. By reinvesting your investment earnings, your initial investment can then enjoy the magical benefits of compound earnings.

If you're also willing to make regular contributions to your super account, or other investments, then your investment portfolio will double in value in super-quick time, assuming the investment markets are performing well. You can also lose money when investing. Anyone with a superannuation account can probably recall the negative investment returns (investment losses) suffered by most Australian super fund members during 2008 and 2009. Over the longer term, however, you can expect a typical super account to deliver positive and decent returns.

Example 1: double your money

Renee has deposited **$5000** in a savings account earning 7 per cent in interest each year, or $350 in interest each year. If Renee leaves her $5000 in the savings account for five years, but chooses to spend her interest each year, she will still have **$5000** in her savings account at the end of five years, but she won't have accumulated any more wealth (see example 1 in table 3.1). In fact, because of inflation (rising prices), her $5000 will buy her less in five years' time than she can buy with her $5000 today. If, however, Renee reinvested her annual interest, she would have more money at the end of the five years. You might think Renee's savings account would then total **$6750** ($5000 plus five years worth of $350 annual interest). Not so! Renee's balance after five years of reinvesting interest totals **$7013**, due to the effects of compound earnings: she has earned interest on her interest. Ignoring tax, if Renee then reinvests her earnings for another five years she can nearly double her original investment from $5000 to **$9835**—just under $10 000 (see example 1 in table 3.1).

Example 2: double your super money

Now let's change the story: assume Renee has **$50 000** in a superannuation account and she makes no further contributions to that account for the next 10 years. This scenario is very common for women who take time out of the workforce to raise children. If Renee's superannuation money is invested in assets that deliver 7 per cent return after fees and taxes, then her super account balance will grow to **$98 358**—nearly double her original balance after 10 years (see example 2 in table 3.1), and double again to nearly **$200 000** after another 10 years, and double again to nearly **$400 000** after another 10 years, growing to nearly **$750 000** after 40 years—if she still hasn't withdrawn her retirement savings after 40 years.

Table 3.1: watch Renee's savings grow*

Year	Example 1†		Example 2
	$5000 savings account		$50 000 super account
	Earning 7%		Earning 7%
	Withdraw interest	Reinvest interest	Reinvest earnings
	$	$	$
Start of year 1	5000	5000	50000
End of year			
1	5000	5350	53500
2	5000	5725	57245
3	5000	6125	61252
4	5000	6554	65540
5	**5000**	**7013**	**70128**
6	5000	7504	75037
7	5000	8029	80289
8	5000	8591	85909
9	5000	9192	91923
10	**5000**	**9835**	**98358**
End of year			
20	5000	19347	**193470**
30	5000	38058	**380580**
40	5000	74867	**748670**

* The amounts for future years are in future dollars: the figures are not in today's dollars.
† In example 1, we have ignored the tax payable on interest income.

Tip

Throughout this book, I use 7 per cent after fees and taxes as the assumed rate of return in most of the superannuation case studies and examples. For ease of comparison, I have also used a return of 7 per cent for the savings account example in table 3.1. although, as at June 2011, the at-call interest rate on cash accounts was about 5 per cent, and around 6 per cent for a term deposit.

Aiming for higher return means greater risk

In example 2, I have assumed an annual return on Renee's superannuation account of 7 per cent after fees and taxes because that is typically the expected long-term return on what is called a balanced investment option. Most Australians have their superannuation money in a balanced investment option, which usually involves a larger portion of shares, property and other higher risk assets, and a smaller portion of cash and lower risk investments, such as fixed-interest investments.

The different categories of investments, such as cash, shares and property, are each known as an asset class. How a super fund divvies up your super money into the different asset classes is known as asset allocation, and most super funds let you choose from different asset allocations, such as conservative, balanced, growth, and high growth or aggressive. Your super fund may give these investment options different names, which can be confusing. (See chapter 10 for an explanation of the investment options offered by super funds and examples of typical asset allocations.)

Although I use an earnings rate of 7 per cent after fees and taxes as the assumed rate of return in the examples discussed in this book, you can choose to invest your super in an asset mix (investment option) that produces returns greater than 7 per cent after fees and taxes over the long term, which means that you usually take on greater risk when investing. Typically, higher risk investment options are called growth, high growth or aggressive growth, and some investment options involve investing in only one asset class, such as an Australian or an international shares option.

The general rule is that the higher the return you aim for, the greater the risk you take. By using the free online calculators referred to throughout this book, you can test a different rate of return, higher or lower than 7 per cent, for your investments if you wish.

If you are willing to accept the occasional negative return (investment loss) in the pursuit of higher returns, then the investment world would describe you as having a medium to high tolerance for risk. If you want to avoid suffering any investment losses, then you would need to consider investments that are lower risk but also deliver lower returns over time. If you fit into the more conservative, risk-averse category, then you're likely to be described as having a low tolerance for risk.

Example 3: higher returns mean faster wealth, but more risk

Renee has decided she has a high tolerance for risk, and wants to aim for an investment return of 10 per cent each year on her superannuation money so it can build more quickly while she isn't working, even though that means that she takes on the risk of having a bad investment year or two during the next 10 years. Renee has shifted all of her superannuation money into a high growth investment option in her superannuation fund, which means 90 per cent of her super money will be invested in Australian and international shares, property investments and other higher risk investments, and the remaining 10 per cent will be invested in cash. Let's assume that each year, for the next 10 years, the high growth option delivers a 10 per cent return after fees and taxes. If Renee made no additional super contributions, her starting account balance of **$50 000** nearly doubles after seven years to **$97 000** and reaches **$130 000** after 10 years (see example 3 in table 3.2, overleaf). For Renee, a 3 per cent difference in investment return means a **$30 000** difference in her retirement account balance (compare with example 2 in table 3.2).

Example 4: add more money and compounding works faster

Renee has just been offered a job after several years out of the workforce raising children. She is returning to full-time employment tomorrow, which means that her superannuation account balance of **$50 000** will benefit from the effects of compound earnings *plus* a super boost when her employer makes regular compulsory super contributions (in accordance with her employer's SG obligations). Renee realises that she probably won't have to take as much risk as she thought she needed to take when investing her super money (see example 3 in table 3.2) because she will now have additional money going into her account regularly, which also enjoys the benefits of compound earnings. She decides to keep her super money in the balanced investment option, which we assume will deliver 7 per cent returns after fees and taxes.

For simplicity, let's assume Renee's employer contributes roughly **$5000** in compulsory SG contributions for the year, after super contributions tax of 15 per cent is deducted ($5895 less 15 per cent tax equals $5011), which means her annual salary is around $65 500. At the end of 10 years, Renee's super account balance will be **$170 500** (see example 4 in table 3.2).

Table 3.2: watch Renee's super savings grow faster*

Year	Example 2	Example 3	Example 4	
	$50 000 super account	$50 000 super account	$50 000 super PLUS $5000 super guarantee (SG) contributions each year	
	Earning 7%	Earning 10%	Earning 7%	
	Reinvest earnings $	Reinvest earnings $	Reinvest earnings $	
Start of year 1	50 000	50 000	50 000	
End of year				
1	53 500	55 000	58 863	
2	57 245	60 500	68 167	
3	61 252	66 550	78 122	
4	65 540	73 205	88 774	
5	**70 128**	**80 525**	**100 171**	
6	75 037	88 578	112 366	
7	80 289	**97 436**	125 415	
8	85 909	107 179	139 377	
9	91 923	117 897	154 317	
End of year 10			**9% SG**	**If 12% SG**
Future dollars	**98 500**	**130 000**	**170 500**	**194 000**
Today's dollars	73 000	96 500	134 000	154 500

* The amounts for future years are in future dollars: the figures are not in today's dollars with the exception of year 10. For year 10, I have provided savings amounts in future dollars, and today's dollars, and rounded to nearest $500. Today's dollars are what your future money would be worth if you spent it today (today's dollars are discussed in more detail later in this chapter). The other assumptions used in table 3.2 are set out in the appendix.

Now that's not the end of the story, because $170 500 in 10 years' time is not the same as $170 500 today. In today's dollars, that $170 500 is worth around **$134 000** due to the effect of inflation (assuming annual inflation of 3 per cent).

When the legislation to increase the rate of SG contributions has been passed, Renee's employer will have to contribute the equivalent of 12 per cent (from July 2019, and between 9.25 and 12 per cent from July 2013) of Renee's salary (rather than 9 per cent), which means she can expect a slightly larger final balance than what appears in example 4. For reference, I have included the final amounts if Renee received 12 per cent in super guarantee contributions for the same 10-year period, at the bottom of example 4 in table 3.2. In reality, Renee's super balance will be somewhere between **$170 000** and **$194 000** because she won't receive 12 per cent in SG contributions for the full 10-year period.

Now, time for a short break and a cuppa. See you in a few minutes.

Good news alert no. 2: employer contributions set to jump to 12 per cent

Superannuation guarantee (SG) is the name for the compulsory superannuation contributions that your employer must make to a super fund on your behalf. Way back in 1992, the SG rate was 3 per cent of a worker's salary or wages, but it rose steadily to reach 9 per cent from 2002. The rate is set to rise again, and employers will be required to contribute the equivalent of 12 per cent of an employee's ordinary time earnings from July 2019 (subject to legislation). The rate will increase in small increments, with the first increase to 9.25 per cent taking effect from July 2013, and then increasing in 0.5 per cent increments each year, until it reaches 12 per cent from July 2019. (See chapter 6 for more on the SG.)

Tip

You can use the free ASIC MoneySmart superannuation calculator at your leisure to work out how a change in the level of super contributions, or a change in the level of investment returns, can increase the size of your final super benefit. I explain how to use the ASIC superannuation calculator in the appendix.

Diversification—balancing return with necessary risk

The return (also known as earnings, income or profit) from an investment is only one side of an investment. You also need to think of the risk of an investment—the possibility of losing your money, which many members of super funds experienced during 2008 and 2009. Some investors also count risk as missing out on a higher return on another investment.

Having money in a bank account in Australia is considered a low-risk investment, because you are unlikely to lose money, and an attractive investment for *part* of a person's investment portfolio. An investment portfolio is the collection of investments a person may hold. An example of a possible investment portfolio could be, say, three high-interest bank accounts, two investment properties, and shares in 12 Australian companies listed on the Australian Securities Exchange (ASX).

If you want a return higher than the interest you can earn on a bank account, then any investment you choose will generally hold greater risk than a bank account. Over time, however, it should also deliver you higher returns. Many investments that deliver higher returns can have a bumpy performance from one year to the next, so you generally expect to hold higher risk assets for five years or more so the strong years outweigh the years of not-so-strong performance.

Your super fund also makes investments. Many Australians, and most super funds, expect to invest money in higher risk investments, such as property and shares. Such investments are higher risk because you are investing in businesses or assets that are subject to the ups and downs of economic cycles, and dependent upon the competence of the individuals managing those assets. Over the longer term, property and shares deliver higher returns than cash in a bank, but in some years, property and share investments can lose money.

The challenge is to balance the risk of potentially losing money with the ultimate aim of delivering decent long-term returns. Most investors, including superannuation funds, balance the desire for higher returns with the possibility of losing money, by investing across different asset classes (such as cash, shares and property) and in a variety of assets within these asset classes. This approach to investing is known as diversification. The way you, or your super fund, decide *how* to spread the risk across different assets is known as asset allocation.

Are you still with me? I'm planning to keep the technical talk to a minimum but bear with me for a few moments longer.

Creating and protecting your wealth for retirement

Why would you, or your super fund, bother having an investment if you could lose your money? Why not just have your money sitting in a bank account that's safe, even though it pays no interest or pays only low interest?

Leaving your money in a bank account that pays interest (known as a cash investment) is certainly a legitimate option, but there are probably three main reasons for also considering investing your money in other assets:

- *Protecting the purchasing power of your money.* Inflation, that is, rising prices, can affect the purchasing power of your savings over time. If inflation is running at 4 per cent a year, then your investments need to return at least 4 per cent a year after tax to ensure you protect the real value of your money. An important question to ask is: what can the money you receive in the future buy you in today's dollars? I explain the concept of today's dollars later in this section.

- *Accumulating wealth.* The minimum requirement for any investment plan is to protect the purchasing power of your money. If you want to accumulate wealth, however, the returns you want from your investments over the longer term need to exceed the inflation rate, and exceed any taxes payable on your investment income. I explain the effect of inflation and tax on your superannuation account, and on your life in retirement later in this section.

- *Creating a regular income from your investments.* Once you accumulate your wealth, you're likely to want your savings, including your super-annuation account, to give you a regular income in retirement. The longer you plan to be retired, the larger the lump sum you need to invest upon retirement. (How much is enough and the type of lump sums you can plan for are discussed in chapter 4.)

Living for today—in today's dollars

Think back to the dream that you have for your retirement. If you plan to live off, say, $40 000 a year in retirement, I assume you're talking about what

37

$40 000 a year buys you today, rather than what $40 000 buys you in 10 or 20 years' time. Inflation, that is, rising prices, can affect the purchasing power of your savings over time.

Example 5: let's talk about today's dollars

Claire is a part-time teacher, and she owns a property investment. She lives very happily on **$40 000** a year, so Claire wants to have a similar lifestyle when she retires. What Claire means is that she wants to live off $40 000 a year in today's dollars, that is, what $40 000 can buy her today, rather than what $40 000 can buy her at some time in the future. If the cost of living increases by 10 per cent over a five-year period, then in five years' time it will cost Claire **$44 000** to maintain the lifestyle that $40 000 in today's dollars can buy her (see table 3.3). If inflation was 20 per cent over the five-year period, then Claire would need **$48 000** in five years' time to maintain the lifestyle she has today on $40 000 annual income. The concept of today's dollars can be confusing so feel free to read example 5 a second or third time.

Table 3.3: today's dollars in future dollars—what $40 000 today is worth in five years' time (example 5)

		Calculations
Desired retirement income	$40 000	**$40 000**
Inflation over five-year period	10%	**$4 000**
Future dollars necessary to give $40 000 in today's dollars		**$44 000**

What today's dollars means for anyone planning for their retirement is that if you want to protect the purchasing power of your money you generally need to invest in assets that produce a return that will at least deliver the same amount as the rate of inflation. (In chapter 4, I highlight the importance of using today's dollars when planning for your retirement.)

Successful investing means real returns after tax

I have covered a lot of concepts in this chapter, but the key message is this: if you're able to save money, then you're well on your way to accumulating wealth. From reading this chapter, you now know that saving your money is not the end of the story. Saving money is a good start, but investing your money means your savings are put to work, and investing is the key to accumulating wealth.

Good news alert no. 3: more super, less tax

The income tax that Australians have to pay on investment returns is why superannuation is the most popular way to save for retirement. The maximum tax that you may pay on regular income is 45 per cent, although most Australians pay a maximum of 37 per cent or 30 per cent (for the 2011–12 year) and a maximum of 37 per cent or 32.5 per cent (for 2012–13, subject to the legislation being passed). The maximum tax that you pay on investment earnings in a superannuation fund is 15 per cent, which means that, for anyone who pays more than 15 per cent tax on income (for 2011–12, that's anyone who earns more than $37000, and from 2012–13, that's anyone who earns more than $18200, or $20542 when you take into account the low income tax offset) superannuation can be a tax-effective retirement planning option.

If you pay less than 15 per cent tax on your income (see the appendix for income tax rates), you may be thinking that superannuation is not so super. If you're an employee, your employer's compulsory superannuation contributions are also subject to 15 per cent tax, even when you don't pay 15 per cent tax on your own income. Fortunately, in 2011 the government was planning to introduce a tax rebate system to refund the super tax paid on the super contributions of lower income earners (see chapter 6 for more on the super rules).

You may be thinking: 'Why is she telling me all this guff — what does this have to do with superannuation, retirement planning, or me?' Well, accumulating wealth is not just about choosing good investments, or selecting a super fund that chooses good investments. Accumulating wealth for retirement generally means *what you can afford to buy* with your wealth when you retire. It's also about how much money you give to the taxman along the way.

I want to introduce two more concepts, and I promise they will be the last for this chapter. The two concepts are:

• real returns

• after-tax returns.

A real return is simply the return you get on an investment after you have deducted the effects of inflation. If your bank account pays 4 per cent interest each year, and inflation (also known as the increase in the Consumer Price

Index, or CPI) is increasing at 4 per cent each year, your savings have retained their purchasing power, but they won't be growing in real terms. If you want your savings and investments to retain their purchasing power over time *and* grow in real terms, then you will need to ensure that the return on your investments exceeds the rate of inflation.

> ## Tip
>
> I must warn you that the remaining pages of this chapter are considerably more complex than the rest of this book. I encourage you to continue reading this chapter, rather than skipping it, because if you can appreciate the effects of tax and inflation on how you grow your wealth, you can potentially add tens of thousands of dollars—or even more—to your personal wealth by the time you retire. At the very least, just scan these concepts for now, and return to them later.

Example 6—real returns give you more of today's dollars

Claire, our friend from example 5, has **$20 000** in a high-interest savings account earning 5 per cent a year in interest (see table 3.4). Her income from annual interest on her savings account is $1000, which means Claire's account balance grows to **$21 000** after 12 months. Inflation for the year is 3 per cent, which means Claire's real return, that is, after taking inflation into account, is 2 per cent (5 minus 3). In dollar terms: $1000 interest less $600 (effect of inflation) equals $400. Although Claire's savings account has grown to $21 000, her account is worth **$20 400** in today's dollars (rather than $21 000) in 12 months' time, due to the effect of inflation.

If Claire paid no tax, the good news is that her savings account has maintained its purchasing power, and actually grown in real terms by 2 per cent (see table 3.4). However, like most Australians, it turns out that Claire does indeed pay tax, which reduces her earnings further (see example 7, and table 3.5 on p. 42).

Table 3.4: real return on Claire's investment (example 6)

	Balance	Return	Value in today's dollars
Savings account	$20 000		
Interest income	$1 000	5.0%	
Balance after 1 year	$21 000		
Less inflation	-$600	-3.0%	
			$20 400
Real return	$400	2.0%	

Example 7: what matters is real returns after taxes

Claire earns $40 000 a year from her teaching and from her property investment. More precisely, she has taxable income of $40 000, which is the income the tax office recognises for taking its cut in tax. Enjoying this level of income means Claire must pay 30 per cent income tax (for the 2011–12 financial year) on any additional income that she earns, such as interest on her savings account. Her interest income of **$1 000** is subject to **$300** income tax, which gives her an after-tax return of **$700**, or 3.5 per cent, rather than 5 per cent (see table 3.5, overleaf). If Claire wants to know her *real return after tax*, then she needs to deduct the effect of inflation, *and* deduct the income tax payable on the income. This gets tricky but stay with me. Claire's gross interest is $1000. Her income tax bill is $300. The effect of inflation is 3 per cent, or $600 of her interest income. We then deduct the $300 and $600 from her $1000 interest income, and Claire's real return after tax is **$100**, or 0.5 per cent on the **$20 000** savings account.

Claire has still protected the purchasing power of her money, but only just. If inflation had been zero, her real return after taxes would be 3.5 per cent. If Claire paid less tax, then her after-tax return would be higher, or if Claire paid more tax, her after-tax return would be lower (see the appendix for income tax rates for 2011–12 and later years).

Table 3.5: real return after tax on Claire's investment (example 7)

		Return
Savings account	$20 000	
Interest income	$1 000	5.0%
Balance after 1 year	$2 000	
Less tax bill (30%)	−$300	−1.5%
Balance after tax after 1 year	$20 700	
Return after tax	$700	3.5%
Balance after tax after 1 year	$20 700	
Less effect of inflation	−$600	−3.0%
After-tax value in today's dollars	$20 100	
Real return after tax	$100	0.5%

Chapter 4

Your Six-Step Wealth Check: how much money is enough?

> **Probably the very best thing my earnings have given me is absence of worry. I have not forgotten what it feels like to worry whether you'll have enough to pay the bills. Not to have to think about that any more is the biggest luxury in the world.**
>
> *J K Rowling, author of the best-selling Harry Potter books*

Planning for your life after you finish working is a lot like planning for a holiday — except that you're preparing for a *very* long holiday.

Think about your last holiday. Before you booked your holiday, you probably researched your preferred destination, and imagined the type of holiday you wanted—basic (camping or hostel accommodation), modest (motels, campervan), comfortable (mid-range hotels, serviced apartments, cruises, economy class overseas flights), or luxurious (five-star hotels, luxury cruises, eco-lodges, health resorts, business class overseas flights).

You probably then worked out how much the holiday was going to cost — flights (if any), petrol, food, accommodation and spending money. You may already have saved the money for the holiday, or, if you're like many Australians, you had to work out how you were going to finance the holiday with existing savings and future savings (even when you choose to use a credit card to initially pay for the holiday). In most cases, you probably had to change your saving habits to ensure you could afford the holiday.

Planning for your retirement involves a similar process. Fortunately, retirement planning is made a lot easier in Australia because most Australians receive a helping hand financially in two key ways:

- If you have a job, your employer is making regular compulsory super contributions (known as SG) on your behalf into a superannuation fund for all of your working life. Even if you are not working at the moment, like most women you will have worked at some stage, or will be working in the future, which means you can expect your retirement savings to be helped along by compulsory employer super contributions.

- Around 80 per cent of Australians receive a full, or part, Age Pension when they retire, which means the amount of superannuation and other savings you need for retirement may not be as much as you expect.

Introducing Trish's Six-Step Wealth Check

The most common question that I'm asked about superannuation and retirement is: how much money is enough? What most people are really asking is: what type of income do I need in retirement to have a reasonable lifestyle, and how much money is enough to finance this level of income for the years I will be in retirement?

In Australia, some people pay thousands of dollars to find out the answers to these questions. In this chapter, I help you answer these questions using my Six-Step Wealth Check — and it's free!

My Six-Step Wealth Check is an easy-to-use process that I have created to help Australians improve their lives in retirement. The six steps help you to work out:

- the type of lifestyle you want

- how much money you need to finance this lifestyle

- how you can reach this wealth target by the time you retire.

I believe many women struggle with setting a retirement target because the financial information available in Australia is often presented back to front. In the introduction to this book, I explained that much of the information available on retirement explains the super rules rather than explaining how you can create the retirement lifestyle that you want by *using* the super rules.

Trish's Six-Step Wealth Check

1 *Choose your lifestyle.* What type of lifestyle do you want in retirement? For example, do you want to have a mobile phone and computer, the financial resources to have regular local or international holidays, or the means to entertain and cater for your family at regular get-togethers?

2 *Calculate the cost of your chosen lifestyle.* How much does such a lifestyle cost each week, or annually? I can give you the answer to this question for a modest or comfortable lifestyle courtesy of a fantastic Australian study.

3 *Calculate the lump sum amount needed for your chosen lifestyle in retirement.* Work out how much money you need to have available as a lump sum on retirement for your chosen lifestyle. Don't worry, I provide you with some target lump sums, and I explain the assumptions that I apply when using the free online calculators.

4 *Do a financial stocktake today.* Calculate the amount of super-annuation and savings you have accumulated up until today.

5 *Do a financial stocktake for tomorrow.* Estimate how much superannuation and other savings you can expect to have accumulated when you retire, if you continue your current savings patterns. Again, I explain how free online calculators can help you with this step and I use practical case studies to demonstrate how the process works.

6 *Close the gap.* Take action if a gap exists between how much you have if you continue doing what you're doing, and how much you believe you need when you retire. A slight boost in super contributions today can transform your retirement tomorrow.

Understanding the superannuation rules is very important, and I do explain these rules (see chapters 6, 10 and 11), but my main objective in this book is to give you practical tools to help you create the retirement lifestyle you want.

Step 1: Choose your lifestyle—what type of life do you want in retirement?

We all have dreams about what our life is going to be like after we finish work, although for many Australians our ability to finance those dreams may be complicated by child-rearing, repaying the mortgage, financing child-related activities, or caring for elderly parents. Depending on your relationship, you may also be the main care-giver to your significant other, which may limit the time you can spend on creating your retirement dream.

In chapter 1, I list some fantastic retirement plans, ranging from living a simple life where you can pay your everyday bills without worrying, and extending through to a retirement where annual overseas trips are the norm.

What one woman considers to be a modest lifestyle may be a luxurious lifestyle for another, depending on a person's current circumstances and level of income. For example, eating out one night a week may be a luxury for a single mum, or for a couple paying off a mortgage and raising children, while it may be considered part of a modest lifestyle by a single woman working full time and earning a high income.

Your retirement lifestyle can also change over time—in the first 10 or 15 years of your retirement you may intend to do all the activities on that list reserved for 'when you retire'. What this can mean is that the lifestyle you have when you're 65 may be very different from your lifestyle when you're 80. In most cases, however, other costs, such as increasing health expenses, may replace some of the money earmarked for leisure, travel and entertainment.

Although lifestyle is a subjective term and each woman reading this will have a unique lifestyle in mind, the one common requirement of all retirement lifestyles is that you must at least cover basic living costs.

For most women, working out the *type* of lifestyle they want in retirement involves working out *how much* their preferred lifestyle is going to cost. The good news is that an Australian study, known as the ASFA Retirement Standard, has worked out the costs of a modest lifestyle and a comfortable lifestyle. I take you through this study and what you can expect from a modest and comfortable lifestyle in step 2.

Why are today's dollars so important?

I explain today's dollars and the importance of maintaining your purchasing power in chapter 3, but for readers who skip or scan chapter 3, I want to highlight the concept of today's dollars.

Future amounts are relatively meaningless when working out how much is enough, unless you can relate the future amounts to what you spend today, which is why, throughout this book, you will read figures expressed in today's dollars. Due to the effects of rising prices over time (inflation), amounts quoted need to be adjusted to what your money can buy today, to make it easy to compare different lifestyles, or to compare the outcomes of using different superannuation strategies. For example, if you're hoping to live on, say, $45000 a year when you retire, I'm certain that you're thinking about what $45000 can buy you in today's dollars and not what $45000 can buy you in 10, 15 or 20 years' time.

Step 2: Calculate the cost of your chosen lifestyle— how much does such a lifestyle cost each week, or each year?

Some expenses will disappear in retirement, such as mortgage repayments (hopefully), child-related expenses and superannuation contributions (unless you're planning to continue working and contribute to super during your retirement), which means you may not need as much income in retirement as you first thought.

You can calculate the cost of your desired lifestyle in retirement using many different methods. For example you can choose to:

- *Use a rough guide.* Say, plan for 65 to 80 per cent of your current gross salary as your desired retirement income. Gross salary is your salary before income tax is deducted. I explain how the rough guide works later in this section, and I use a real-life case study to illustrate the rough guide method in chapter 5.

- *Be specific.* You can estimate what your actual life currently costs per week, and what you expect your life to cost in retirement.

- *Choose a modest or comfortable lifestyle, or something in between.* The ASFA Retirement Standard measures the cost of a modest or comfortable lifestyle in retirement (the Retirement Standard is explained on p. 52).

- *Reach for the stars.* If you're aspiring to a lifestyle that is more than modest or comfortable, then you can set your own target using a percentage of your current salary as a rough guide, or estimating the specific costs of your desired lifestyle. You can then check out chapter 8 for some majestic savings targets. Before you head to chapter 8, I recommend you read this chapter for a short course in my Six-Step Wealth Check.

Use a rough guide

An important message to take from this book is simply this: start planning for your retirement. You don't have to be scientific about your financial security, but I suggest you set yourself a realistic target and make plans to reach that target. The Six-Step Wealth Check is a flexible tool to suit any personality, including those women who don't like budgets, numbers or even detail.

One of the easiest ways to set yourself a retirement savings target is to base it on a percentage of your current income. You may choose a retirement target based on your gross (before-tax) income, or a target based on your annual after-tax income:

- *Before-tax income.* A school of thought within the financial services industry is that you need a minimum of 65 per cent and potentially up to 80 per cent of your pre-retirement income to enjoy your current lifestyle in retirement. For example, if you earn $60 000 a year, then your preferred income in retirement may be between $39 000 and $48 000 a year based on this rough guide.

- *After-tax income.* You may consider that a target based on *after-tax* salary is a more accurate guide for your future retirement lifestyle; such as 65 to 80 per cent of your after-tax salary, or even 80 to 100 per cent of your after-tax salary, or some other variation of these percentages. I show how this rough guide can work in practice in the case study in chapter 5.

Be specific—actual living expenses

The be specific approach is well-suited for those women who like to be organised and need a well-documented plan when embarking on exciting new projects. For other women, doing a tally of your weekly expenses may seem like a drag and too much hard work, but I encourage you to give it a go. You may be surprised by what you spend, and what you won't necessarily be spending when you retire. Some of your living costs are likely to disappear in retirement, such as child-related costs and travel expenses for work.

Good news alert no. 4: if you earn less than $30 000

If you earn less than $30 000 a year and you're living within your means on this income, then a more realistic retirement target is likely to be 80 per cent to 100 per cent of your current *after-tax* income, rather than 65 per cent or some other rough guide. Although everyone's circumstances differ, on $30 000 a year, most of your income is likely to be used for everyday living costs, and generally speaking, many of those costs are likely to continue in retirement.

For example, if you currently earn **$30 000** a year, then 100 per cent of your after-tax income is **$26 400** (for the 2011–12 year), and 80 per cent of your after-tax income is **$21 120**, ignoring any tax rebates you may receive. In fact, a retirement income of $21 120 is very close to the annual income necessary to finance a modest lifestyle in retirement.

The good news is that a retirement income representing 80 per cent of your current after-tax income ($21 120 for 2011–2012) is achievable with **$35 000** in super savings including access to the full Age Pension, and 100 per cent of your current after-tax income ($26 400, for 2011–12) is achievable with about **$110 000** in super savings, including access to the full Age Pension. If you're hoping for a better lifestyle than you now have, or a better than modest lifestyle, then that can be possible too, but it may not happen automatically. A worthwhile exercise is to be specific about your current expenses: actually work out how much you spend each week, or each year, and then determine your preferred retirement income on this basis (see table 4.1 on p. 51).

The key to wealth accumulation is usually not about how much you earn but the willingness to take action, invest wisely, and to make regular contributions over time.

Your tally doesn't have to be exact—just an estimate. In table 4.1, start with your current expenses, and then think about what your expenses would be in retirement. For example, work out your essential expenses, and then add your discretionary expenses such as leisure (holiday travel, entertainment) and alcohol. Although the cost of living will change by the time you retire, the table looks at costs in today's dollars—what you expect your retirement expenses would be, based on what they cost *now*. The exercise can be very illuminating, and may even help you with managing your lifestyle today.

The last column of table 4.1 contains the Age Pension amount you can expect per week (paid fortnightly), if you were entitled to the full Age Pension when you retire. If you have no savings or superannuation when you retire, the Age Pension amount (which is indexed over time in line with increasing prices) is what you would be forced to live on, assuming you've reached Age Pension age. If you were born on or after 1 January 1957 you can access the Age Pension only when you turn 67. If you were born before July 1952 your Age Pension age is 65 or, in specified cases, younger than 65. If you were born before 1957 but after June 1952 then you can only get the Age Pension when you turn 65.5, 66, or 66.5 years (see chapter 11).

Is the weekly cost of your expected retirement lifestyle higher than the weekly rate of Age Pension? If you believe that your expected weekly retirement costs can be covered by **$365** a week, or around **$18 960** a year for a single woman in today's dollars (the Age Pension rate for singles in June 2011 — indexed every six months in line with increasing prices), then you're in a fairly comfortable position retirement-wise. If you're part of a couple, then you can also use table 4.1 to work out your actual living costs, and compare them with the Age Pension rate. In June 2011, the weekly Age Pension amount for a couple was **$550** (or around **$28 590** over a year).

For most women, however, the lifestyle expectations for retirement exceed what you can expect to receive in Age Pension entitlements, even when you take into account special pensioner discounts and rebates. Fortunately, most Australian women have some superannuation savings as a starting point, but there is usually a gap between what you want in retirement, and what you can achieve with your existing savings habits. The Six-Step Wealth Check can help you identify when your retirement expectations don't match your current retirement reality, and provide you with some options to close the expectation gap.

As a first step, fill in table 4.1 to estimate your current living expenses.

Choose a modest or comfortable lifestyle, or something in between

In the past, the trickiest aspect of retirement planning has been the uncertainty surrounding how much it actually costs to live in retirement. Table 4.1 is an attempt to look into the future based on your current lifestyle, but wouldn't it be great if you had access to research that measured the cost of living for actual retirees? What we need is research that measures what minimum income is required to deliver a woman a decent life in retirement. Well, I have great news! I can provide you with hard data on how much it costs to finance a modest or comfortable lifestyle in retirement.

Table 4.1: your weekly expenses*

	Current (today) $	In retirement $	Age Pension[†] $
Housing costs (e.g. home loan, rates, maintenance)			
Personal loans and credit card repayments			
Electricity, gas, water			
Food			
Clothing and footwear (including cleaning and clothing repairs)			
Household goods and services (including telephone, house insurance)			
Health (e.g. medical, dental, health insurance)			
Transport (including car expenses, car insurance)			
School fees			
Entertainment, leisure, holiday travel (including cost of dining out)			
Personal care (including hair cuts, facials, make-up)			
Gifts, tobacco, alcohol			
Other items not covered above			
Total costs			365[†] a week (single) 550[†] a week (couple)

* If you receive annual bills, divide the expense by 52 to work out weekly expense. If you pay a bill monthly, then multiply the bill by 12, then divide by 52 to work out weekly expense. If you pay a quarterly bill, multiply by 4 to determine the annual bill, then divide by 52 to work out the weekly expense.
† Age Pension rate as at March 2011, and adjusted each year in March and September. Payments are made fortnightly, although the rates quoted in table 4.1 have been converted to weekly amounts. The Age Pension rate quoted includes the Age Pension supplement, and are the latest rates available as at June 2011. For the latest rates visit <www.superguide.com.au> or <www.centrelink.gov.au>.

The ASFA Retirement Standard measures the cost of a modest or comfortable lifestyle in retirement, in weekly and in annual amounts. (ASFA stands for the Association of Superannuation Funds of Australia, one of the largest superannuation industry associations.) For the rest of the book, I will refer to this study as the Retirement Standard.

Tip

The Retirement Standard assumes that you own your own home, and that you pay no tax on your income. For many Australians entering retirement, tax will not be an issue due to the tax incentives associated with superannuation and also the special tax rebates applicable to older Australians. If you do end up paying tax in retirement, then treat the figures quoted in the next section as after-tax income. (Tax rules in retirement are explained in chapter 11.)

Originally released in 2004 and revamped in 2010, the Retirement Standard is based on the lives of actual retirees living in Australia, and the income amounts are adjusted every three months in line with the cost of living. This fantastic study means you now have a relevant and tangible savings target for retirement, and a reasonable idea of what income you need for a modest or comfortable lifestyle (see table 4.2 on p. 59). For comparison and completeness, I have added a third lifestyle — basic — which represents living solely on the Age Pension.

Cleaner future means tax cuts and more Age Pension

In July 2011 the federal government announced a clean energy and carbon pricing policy that will tax the biggest polluting companies in Australia. The cost of this carbon tax is expected to be passed on to consumers in the form of higher prices, which may increase the cost of living in the future. As a means of offsetting the possible cost increases for consumers, the government is introducing substantial tax cuts from July 2012 (see the appendix), and also introducing a clean energy supplement for people on the Age Pension and other retirees (subject to legislation being passed — see chapter 11).

How much does a modest or comfortable lifestyle cost?

According to the Retirement Standard, assuming you own your own home, you need the following amounts of money, after tax, to give you a modest or comfortable lifestyle:

- *Modest lifestyle ($21 132 a year, or $30 557 for a couple).* Expect an after-tax income that is slightly more than the Age Pension. Such an income gives you a better lifestyle than living solely on the Age Pension, but you generally can only afford basic activities. The modest lifestyle figures assume you take out private health cover, and also allows about $10 a week (and $16 a week for a couple) for the costs of a bundled home phone, mobile phone and internet connection. Overseas trips are generally out of the question, but not entirely impossible if you're willing to give up other items. The good news for some is that the modest lifestyle allows $10 a week for alcohol (and $15 a week for a couple).

- *Comfortable lifestyle ($39 302 a year, or $53 729 for a couple).* According to the Retirement Standard, a comfortable lifestyle enables 'an older, healthy retiree to be involved in a broad range of leisure and recreational activities and to have a good standard of living through the purchase of such things as: household goods, private health insurance, a reasonable car, good clothes, a range of electronic equipment, and domestic and occasionally international holiday travel'. (ASFA <www.superannuation. asn.au/RS/default.aspx>.) Lovely!

However, a comfortable life is not necessarily a luxurious life. I chat about what to do if you want a *very* comfortable (or some may say luxurious) life later in the chapter.

You can also consider living what I call a basic lifestyle: that is, living solely on the Age Pension. At the time of writing, Centrelink, the government body that administers the Age Pension, paid eligible Australians around **$18 960** a year (single) or around **$28 590** a year (for a couple), including a pension supplement. The Age Pension is adjusted twice a year, in line with inflation, in March and September. The single Age Pension, excluding the pension supplement, represents 27.7 per cent of total average weekly earnings for males. In 2011 total average weekly earnings for males were about **$64 000** a year.

Some retired Australians live happily on the Age Pension, but a vast majority of these contented individuals retired before the explosion of technology — mobile phones, laptops, the internet, digital cameras, plasma screens and the list goes on. Relying solely on the Age Pension can deliver you a basic income and access to discounts on health services and energy costs.

Although I do believe Australia's Age Pension system is an excellent financial buffer for retirees, very few future retirees expect to live on this level of income by choice.

Tip

From July 2012 a person's Age Pension entitlement will include a clean energy supplement (subject to the legislation being passed). This means that the annual Age Pension amounts, and annual retirement incomes (that include an Age Pension entitlement) quoted in this chapter, and throughout the book, will increase by up to $338 in today's dollars for a single person, and around $510 in today's dollars for a couple, in addition to the regular six-monthly adjustment to the Age Pension rates (see chapter 11 for more detailed information).

What does a comfortable lifestyle provide, that a modest lifestyle can't?

The first question that I'm usually asked whenever I chat about modest or comfortable lifestyles is this: what does a comfortable lifestyle of just over $39 000 a year (for a single person) buy you that a modest lifestyle (just over $21 000 a year) can't?

Good question! Generally speaking, a comfortable lifestyle represents a standard of living among older, healthy and fully active retirees that enables these retirees to enjoy leisure and recreational activities without having to stress about whether they can pay the everyday bills, and without denying themselves basic necessities and home comforts. Yes, that's interesting, but what does that really mean: how does a comfortable lifestyle look on a day-to-day basis?

According to the research behind the Retirement Standard, a comfortable lifestyle, compared with a modest lifestyle, means you can enjoy the following activities:

- *Housing.* You can update your bathroom and kitchen at some stage during your retirement.

- *Energy.* You can afford the extra costs of running an air-conditioner without financial stress.

- *Food/dining out.* You can eat out regularly each week (three nights at an RSL, or one night at a fancier restaurant); have family or friends over for roast dinner once a fortnight; and enjoy a bottle of wine or two (spend around $25 in total each week), or two to four bottles of wine if you're part of a couple (spend around $40 per week).

- *Clothing and footwear.* You can afford more fancy underwear, socks and stockings, and you can spend slightly more on your winter and summer clothing.

- *Household goods and services.* You can replace whitegoods when necessary, and have air-conditioning. You could also invest in a home security system, and have regular pest inspections.

- *Health.* You can afford to take out top rate private health insurance cover.

- *Transport.* You can drive a relatively new car rather than an old jalopy.

- *Leisure.* You can buy magazines, CDs and DVDs. You can use a computer, internet and mobile phone regularly, and own hobby equipment, such as golf clubs and fishing gear. You can enjoy regular holidays in Australia and take off overseas once every five years.

- *Personal care.* According to the research, women living a comfortable lifestyle spend considerably more on hairdressing, cosmetic and personal care items than women living a modest lifestyle.

Tip

The main difference between modest and comfortable lifestyles is the amount of money spent on food, household goods and services, clothing and footwear, transport, health, leisure and alcohol.

If you're still curious about the nitty gritty details of a comfortable (or modest) lifestyle, then you can visit the Retirement Standard section of the ASFA website at <www.superannuation.asn.au/RS/default.aspx>, where you can compare the detailed spending habits of retirees covering around 30 individual items.

Reach for the stars — living on more than $39 000 a year (single) or more than $54 000 a year (couple)

Okay, you may have looked at the income levels quoted for a comfortable lifestyle and thought to yourself: 'That's not my idea of comfortable. I'm earning $80 000 (or $90 000 or more) a year at the moment, and there's no way that I can reduce my expenses to $39 000 a year'.

Your response may certainly reflect your retirement expectations, but if you're currently earning $80 000 a year, then more than **$17 000** of your income is heading to the taxman. Assuming you don't pay tax in retirement (and most Australians don't pay tax if they receive superannuation benefits), the maximum income that you will need in retirement to match a current lifestyle on $80 000 a year is **$62 450** (for 2011–12, or **$62 453** for 2012–13, subject to the legislation being passed — see the appendix for income tax rates).

If you earn $90 000 a year, then more than **$21 000** of your income is heading directly to the taxman. A current lifestyle based on an annual working income of $90 000 a year is the equivalent of an after-tax income of just under **$69 000**.

In addition, you're unlikely to have mortgage repayments or child-related expenses, such as the cost of education, when you retire. Taking the removal of these costs into account, you may be pleasantly surprised by what your retirement lifestyle will cost. Even so, if you're making comments similar to the one above, then keep on reading. Perhaps you want a very comfortable life, or maybe you're aspiring to a luxurious life in retirement.

One drawback with the Retirement Standard is that it doesn't measure the costs of a lifestyle that is more than comfortable, or what some women may call a luxurious lifestyle. Interestingly, the issue that seems to trigger the biggest reaction when discussing the Retirement Standard study is the fact that only $25 a week for a single person and $40 a week for a couple is allocated to alcohol each week in the comfortable lifestyle. Another big concern for those wanting a higher standard of living is the fact that the comfortable lifestyle allows for overseas travel every five years with an average cost allowed of just under $10 000 per trip for a single, and $14 000 for a couple (average cost of $1900 a year for a single person or $2800 a year for a couple), when some budding retirees imagine leaving on a jet plane at least every second year, and hopefully every year.

The Retirement Standard's comfortable lifestyle is merely indicative and you may swap some of the expenditure for other items, because each person's priorities are different for retirement. For example, you may not run a car in retirement, preferring to spend that money on more frequent or longer overseas holidays.

If you do want a lifestyle that is grander than the Retirement Standard considers comfortable, then planning now for the lifestyle you want in retirement takes on a greater urgency. By working through my Six-Step Wealth Check, you can better appreciate the level of income that you'll need for the lifestyle that you want, and how you can reach your savings target.

In chapter 8, I apply the Six-Step Wealth Check for those wanting an annual income in retirement that exceeds $39 000 for a single person and $54 000 for a couple. But don't leave this chapter just yet! You may decide that a comfortable lifestyle is an attractive option by the time you finish reading chapter 4.

Step 3: Calculate the lump sum amount needed for your chosen lifestyle — your retirement savings target

The short story of retirement planning is this: if you want to live on more than the Age Pension, then you need to accumulate wealth through your superannuation account or by growing your non-superannuation savings, or both.

Even when you retire, your superannuation money must be invested to finance your income stream (pension) for the rest of your life. In step 3, you can work out how much money (savings) you need on retirement to finance your preferred level of income, assuming that the lump sum (or target retirement amount) is invested at a certain rate of return. Throughout this book, the assumed rate of return that I use for most examples is 7 per cent after fees and taxes. (See chapter 3 for my rationale for using this rate of return.)

Table 4.2 on p. 59 lists the lump sum amounts that you need to invest (or your super fund invests on your behalf) when you retire to deliver a modest or comfortable lifestyle. I have used two handy financial calculators created by ASIC — the MoneySmart retirement planner and the MoneySmart account-based pension calculators — to calculate the lump sum amounts.

The key messages that you can take from table 4.2 are:

- *Age Pension only.* If you retire with no savings, then you can expect to live solely on the Age Pension, which is just under **$19 000** a year for a single person, and around **$28 600** for a couple.

- *Modest lifestyle.* As a single person, you need only **$35 000** in superannuation savings to create a retirement income of $21 132 a year (including a full Age Pension). As a couple, you only need **$33 000** in super savings to create a retirement income of $30 557 a year (including a full Age Pension).

- *Modest lifestyle with no Age Pension.* If you're not eligible for the Age Pension, then, as a single person, you will need **$320 000** in super when you retire to finance an annual retirement income of $21 132. A couple will need **$465 000** in super savings to finance an annual income of $30 557. Circumstances where you may not be eligible for the Age Pension include retiring before you reach Age Pension age, or when the value of your total assets (excluding your home) exceed the Age Pension asset limits. (See chapter 11 for how the Age Pension rules work.)

- *Comfortable lifestyle.* As a single person, you need at least **$400 000** in super savings to finance an annual retirement income of $39 302 (including a part Age Pension). As a couple, you need at least **$465 000** in super savings to finance a retirement income of $53 729 a year (including a part Age Pension).

- *Comfortable lifestyle with no Age Pension.* If you're not eligible for the Age Pension, then you will need **$595 000** in super on retirement as a single person to create a comfortable lifestyle on $39 302 a year. With no Age Pension entitlements, a couple will need **$820 000** in super savings to finance an annual income of $53 729.

Step 4: Do a financial stocktake today

Step 4 of my Six-Step Wealth Check—conduct a financial stocktake—is reasonably straightforward. You locate all of your superannuation accounts and then you count up the value of all of the superannuation that you currently have. You then do the same with your other savings and investments (if any)—cash, term deposits, shares, investment properties. (Chapter 10 has tips on how to find lost super.)

Table 4.2: how much super is enough for a modest or comfortable lifestyle?

| Lifestyle | Single | | | Couple | | |
| | Annual income $ | Target lump sum on retirement $ | | Annual income $ | Target lump sum on retirement $ | |
		No Age Pension	Receives Age Pension		No Age Pension	Receives Age Pension
Basic (Age Pension)	18 962	Not applicable	Nil	28 585	Not applicable	Nil
Modest	21 132	320 000	$35 000 plus full Age Pension	30 557	465 000	$33 000 plus full Age Pension
Comfortable	39 302	595 000	At least $400 000 but less than $595 000	53 729	820 000	At least $465 000 but less than $820 000

Notes:

• The lump sum amounts are calculated using the ASIC MoneySmart account-based pension calculator and the ASIC MoneySmart retirement planner calculator. The lump sum amounts are in today's dollars and assume retirement at the age of 65, or at age 67.

• The annual incomes listed in table 4.2 last for 22 years (until age 87 if the individual retires at 65, and until age 89, if individual retires at age 67).

• If you hope to claim the Age Pension in retirement, you must have reached your Age Pension age (ranging from 65 to 67, depending on your birth date). Anyone born before July 1952 has an Age Pension age of 65 or younger, while anyone born on or after 1 January 1957 has an Age Pension age of 67 years (see chapter 11).

• The lump sums are reinvested in the superannuation system throughout retirement.

• Income tax is not reflected in table 4.2, because the amounts assume annual income is taken as an income stream (pension) from a superannuation fund, which is tax-free at or after the age of 60 (see chapters 6 and 11). In many cases, tax is not relevant for retirees even when an individual holds investments outside the super system, due to the level of income received by the individual and the special income tax rates available for eligible older Australians.

• Other assumptions used in table 4.2 are listed in the appendix.

Step 5: Do a financial stocktake for tomorrow

Now calculate how much superannuation and other savings and investments you can expect to have when you retire, if you continue doing exactly what you're doing now.

ASIC produces several nifty financial calculators, but the calculator most useful for step 5 of my Six-Step Wealth Check is ASIC's MoneySmart superannuation calculator.

You need the following information to use the MoneySmart superannuation calculator:

• your age

• your expected retirement age

- your annual income

- how much super you have today (current balance)

- how much you plan to contribute (if any) to your super account from today until you retire.

It's easier than it sounds because ASIC's MoneySmart superannuation calculator does most of the work for you. You type in your age, your expected retirement age, your annual income and your current super balance. You then answer 'yes' or 'no' to the question: 'Do you make voluntary contributions?' If the answer is 'yes', you type in the amount you intend to contribute each year, until a certain age, or until you retire.

I show how step 5 and the calculator operate in practice in chapter 5, where I take you through a case study inspired by real life, and in the case studies throughout this book (chapters 5, 7, and 9).

Tip

The MoneySmart superannuation calculator does not automatically cater for women who intend to take a break from employment at any time between now and when they intend to retire. You have to do more than one calculation on the calculator to deliver outcomes if you plan to or have taken work breaks. Some super funds do provide free online calculators that can help you with this calculation. You could check with your super fund to see if your fund provides such a calculator on its website. Alternatively, you can ask your superannuation fund, or an adviser connected to your super fund, or a general financial adviser to help you with this exercise. The case studies in chapters 7 and 9 include calculations for women taking breaks from paid employment.

Step 6: Close your retirement gap

Now, we have reached the business end of the Six-Step Wealth Check, and you have thought about the following:

- the type of lifestyle that you want in retirement (step 1)

- how much that lifestyle will cost you each year (step 2)

- the lump sum amount needed for your chosen lifestyle in retirement (step 3)

- what you currently have in superannuation and other savings (step 4)

- what your current savings can deliver you, in terms of a lump sum, if you continue what you've been doing in the past (step 5).

Tip

For simplicity, it's often easier to use the Six-Step Wealth Check primarily to track your superannuation savings, and then at a later time focus on any non-super savings or investments you may have. ASIC also provides a free online calculator that you can use to estimate how your existing non-super savings have grown. The MoneySmart compound interest calculator can estimate what your non-super savings will be worth at a future date if you reinvest all the interest you earn. The calculator can estimate for a one-off amount, or for an investment where you make regular additional investments. The one flaw with the compound interest calculator is that it doesn't take into account fees and taxes, although you can correct this flaw fairly easily by inserting into the calculator the assumed investment return after fees and taxes (the appendix has more tips on using the MoneySmart calculators). A financial adviser can also help with this calculation.

You have chosen your preferred lifestyle and you now know whether your existing savings patterns will deliver the lifestyle you want. Is there a gap between what you aspire to in retirement and what your actual savings and investment habits will deliver? Congratulations if the answer is 'no', that is, your expectations can be met by your actual savings and investment habits. For most of you, however, there's likely to be a gap between the amount of savings that you'll need for your chosen lifestyle, and the amount of savings you'll have if you continue your current savings patterns.

If a gap exists between how much you have if you continue doing what you're doing and how much you believe you need when you retire, then you generally have four main options:

- *Save more for your retirement.* Chapter 10 has 15 tips on how to boost your superannuation savings. The case studies in chapters 5, 7 and 9 illustrate how even a slight boost in super contributions can transform your final retirement payout.

- *Delay retirement to enable you to accumulate more superannuation and other savings.* By working longer, you can enter retirement with a larger lump sum, *and* your retirement savings will have to finance fewer years in retirement. For example, if you retire at age 55, you will need to finance a retirement of around 30 years (on average), and you won't have access to the Age Pension until you reach at least the age of 65. If you retire at age 65, rather than age 55, you can expect a retirement lasting 22 years (on average), which means you will need a smaller lump sum on retirement for the same level of income, because you're financing fewer years in retirement.

- *Lower your retirement lifestyle expectations.* You don't have to make this decision yet! Consider some of the strategies to boost your super and then think about your retirement options.

- *A combination of two or more of the above options.*

Chapter 5

Case study—I'm 52. Is it too late to start saving?

> *Women's education is almost more important than the education of boys and men. We—and by 'we' I do not mean only we in India but all the world—have neglected women's education.*
>
> *Indira Gandhi, former Prime Minister of India*

I answer many questions from readers on my free consumer website, SuperGuide at <www.superguide.com.au>, and one of the most popular questions is: 'how much money is enough?' In chapter 4 we saw my Six-Step Wealth Check, and in this chapter I demonstrate how my Six-Step Wealth Check works using a case study.

The key message that I would like you to take from this case study is this: it is never too late to improve your financial circumstances, and it's possible to dramatically change your lifestyle in retirement by taking action now.

Irene's story: the facts

Irene is 52 years old and has just paid off the home loan on her two-bedroom unit. Irene believes that she is grossly unprepared for her retirement. Irene is also worried that she has left it too late to save for retirement and that she will end up struggling financially when she finishes work. She intends to retire at age 65, claim the Age Pension and hopefully take a small income stream from her superannuation fund. She earns $39 000 a year and her employer contributes 9 per cent in SG contributions each year of $3510, paid into her super fund in quarterly instalments.

Irene's financial future is better than she believes:

- Irene is pleasantly surprised to discover that she has $35 000 in her super account, simply for doing nothing but turning up for work.

- Even if Irene does nothing but turn up for work each day, she will still enjoy a better than modest lifestyle in retirement with minimal planning.

- Now that Irene has paid off her unit, she doesn't have to budget for mortgage repayments, and so she has a spare $200 a week to spend or save.

- She can start paying $100 a week in voluntary superannuation contributions without any trouble.

It's amazing what a little planning can do. If Irene can make a $100 super contribution each week, starting now and continuing until she retires, she can expect a lifestyle in retirement similar to, if not better than, the current lifestyle she leads.

Age Pension: is it 65 or 67?

Around 80 per cent of Australian retirees receive a full or part Age Pension, and Irene, like most Australians, can expect her retirement plans to include a substantial Age Pension, if not a full Age Pension.

According to Irene's plan, she has 13 years (from the age of 52) to accumulate superannuation savings before she intends to retire at the age of 65. The Age Pension is clearly an important part of Irene's retirement plans, which means she will need to reconsider her retirement date. Due to the year that she was born, Irene will not be able to access the Age Pension until she turns 67. Irene was born after December 1956, which means her Age Pension age is 67 years (see the tip box on p. 65).

Irene must now plan for retirement in 15 years' time rather than 13 years, since she is relying on the Age Pension for a substantial portion of her retirement income.

> ## Tip
>
> The Age Pension age is 67 for anyone born on or after 1 January 1957. The Age Pension age is between 65.5 years and 66.5 years for anyone born on or after 1 July 1952 and before 1 January 1957. Anyone born before 1 July 1952 has an Age Pension age of 65 or younger (see chapter 11 for more detailed information).

Irene's Six-Step Wealth Check—how a little effort can make a huge difference

Now, I have to say a few words of warning before I can continue with Irene's exciting journey towards financial security in retirement. The case study is merely an illustration of what an individual may choose to do when saving for retirement, and it should be treated as information of a general nature. If you're thinking seriously about retirement you should do your own research on your financial needs. Anyone thinking seriously about making financial decisions for retirement should consider seeking tax advice and, if necessary, retirement planning advice (see chapter 12). Now, back to Irene's story.

Steps 1 and 2: What type of lifestyle do you want in retirement, and how much will that retirement cost?

Irene is already better placed for her retirement than many other Australians of similar age because she has paid off her home unit and will enter retirement debt-free. Even better, Irene now has surplus money that she can redirect to her retirement savings.

Irene needs to think about the type of lifestyle that she wants, and can afford, when she eventually retires.

Does Irene want a modest or comfortable lifestyle?

Irene uses the ASFA Retirement Standard (see chapter 4) as a benchmark for the possible lifestyle she can enjoy when she finishes working. The Retirement Standard is based on the lives of actual retirees, and indicates that a modest lifestyle for a single person costs **$21 132** a year, and a comfortable lifestyle costs **$39 302** a year for a single person.

> **Tip**
>
> The income and cost levels quoted for the modest and comfortable lifestyles are after-tax income. If someone holds their money in the super system, no tax is payable on most super benefits after the age of 60.

Briefly, a modest lifestyle is better than living solely on the Age Pension, but you can afford only basic activities, and no luxuries. You can afford private health cover, but the modest lifestyle allows only for a basic internet and mobile phone service, and allocates $10 a week for alcohol. A comfortable lifestyle (compared with a modest lifestyle) lets you eat out reasonably regularly, take out the top rate of private health insurance cover, visit a hairdresser regularly, use the internet and mobile phone more, drive a relatively new car, drink more alcohol or better quality alcohol, have an overseas holiday every five years, and enjoy frequent Australian holidays.

Irene may be hoping for a lifestyle closer to comfortable — which is actually better than her current lifestyle even though she earns $39 000 — nearly the same income level necessary for a comfortable life in retirement. How can Irene expect a better lifestyle on the same level of income? Ah, but this is where our tax system comes into play!

Irene can say goodbye to income tax

Irene won't need to aim for the same level of income in retirement to deliver the same lifestyle that she enjoys now. Irene currently pays **$5250** in income tax on her $39 000 annual income (for 2011–12, or **$4222** in income tax for 2012–13, subject to the legislation being passed), which means the after-tax income that she lives on today is a lot less than $39 000. Ignoring the low income tax offset Irene receives, her after-tax income works out to be **$33 750** (for 2011–12 year, or **$34 778** for 2012–13, subject to the legislation being passed — see the appendix for income tax rates).

In retirement, Irene won't be paying tax if she keeps her savings in the super system, and will pay very little tax (if any) if she has her savings outside the super system. Further, she is no longer paying a mortgage, and in retirement she will no longer have work-related expenses, and won't be making super contributions (although she may choose to continue working and contributing to super for part of her retirement).

Tip

Assuming all other expenditure remains the same (although it is likely some of Irene's living costs will disappear in retirement), if Irene chose to aim for a tax-free retirement income of **$39 000** (for 2011–12), then that equates to a working income of **$46 000** before tax (for the 2011–12 year)—much higher than her current income. Irene didn't think about the impact of tax until now, and she realises that her target retirement income can be much lower than $39 000 to still be able to enjoy the lifestyle she has today.

Irene considers three different income measures

For Irene to truly compare what type of income she needs to maintain her lifestyle in retirement, she could use many different measures. Here are three possible measures:

- *Current after-tax working income.* Irene's **$39 000** before-tax income translates into an after-tax income of **$33 750** (for the 2011–12 year), before taking into account the low income tax offset she will also receive later in chapter.

- *80 per cent of current before-tax income.* A popular rule-of-thumb when working out your retirement income needs is to assume that retirement lifestyle costs are between 65 per cent and 80 per cent of your pre-retirement lifestyle costs. Aiming for an income target that is less than your current income recognises that you're unlikely to be repaying a mortgage in retirement, unlikely to be making super contributions, and hopefully living a life with little or no tax. Irene's income is already below the average income for an Australian worker of around **$66 000**, and just under the average working income of around **$41 000** for an Australian female, so Irene is likely to aim towards the higher end, namely 80 per cent. Her target retirement income may then be **$31 200** (80 per cent of **$39 000**). Irene won't pay tax in retirement on income of **$31 200** a year, sourced from superannuation savings and the Age Pension.

- *Aim for the modest or comfortable lifestyle benchmark, or something in between.* Irene may decide to plan for a modest or comfortable lifestyle, or something in between these two lifestyles, as measured by the Retirement Standard (see table 5.1, overleaf).

> ## Tip
>
> Due to the tax concessions available in retirement, an annual retirement income of **$33 750** can be the financial equivalent of **$39 000** (for 2011–12) before retirement.

Step 3: How much money will you need to finance these levels of income?

Table 5.1 lists Irene's possible target retirement incomes and the lump sums necessary on retirement to deliver Irene each level of income.

> ## Tip
>
> In addition to six-monthly adjustments to the Age Pension rates, from July 2012 a person's Age Pension entitlement will include a clean energy supplement (subject to the legislation being passed). (See chapter 11 for more information.) What this means for Irene is that when the Age Pension adjustments take effect, she will need slightly less super to achieve the same annual retirement incomes listed in the following four tables and text.

Table 5.1: how much money is enough for Irene's retirement (from age 67)?

Irene's lifestyle options	Target annual income $	Lump sum needed for income until age 87 $	Lump sum needed for income until age 100 $
Age Pension only	18 962	Nil	Nil
Modest lifestyle	21 132	35 000 plus full Age Pension	55 000 plus full Age Pension
Comfortable lifestyle	39 302	400 000	650 000
Irene's current after-tax working income	33 750	266 000	430 000
80% of Irene's before-tax working income	31 200	210 000	335 000

Note: Lump sum calculations were made using the ASIC MoneySmart retirement planner calculator. For assumptions used in table 5.1, see the appendix.

Step 4: Work out how much superannuation and non-super savings that you have now

Although Irene has paid off her home loan, her only other source of savings is going to be her superannuation account. Since 2002, her employer has paid the equivalent of 9 per cent of her salary in the form of compulsory superannuation contributions (SG) into her superannuation account. Between 1992 and 2002, her employer's contributions increased from 3 to 8 per cent of Irene's salary.

Irene didn't realise that her employer had been contributing for this long, and she is surprised and slightly relieved to discover that she already has **$35 000** in her superannuation account.

Step 5: Estimate how much super and non-super savings you're going to have when you retire

If Irene continues what she's doing, that is, does no retirement planning but still turns up for work as usual, then Irene's employer must continue contributing the equivalent of 9 per cent of her salary to her super account until she retires at age 67.

Irene uses the ASIC MoneySmart superannuation calculator to find out how much she will have when she reaches 67 in 15 years' time. Her compulsory employer contributions (less contributions tax) plus investment earnings will deliver her **$174 000** (in tomorrow's dollars), which works out to be **$122 000** (in today's dollars), starting from her initial balance of $35 000. The future account balance is **$174 000**, but when adjusted for inflation over the 15-year period works out at **$122 000** in today's dollars (see table 5.2, overleaf). Today's dollars means that the superannuation calculator takes into account the effects of cost-of-living increases (assumed to be 3 per cent a year) and works out what Irene's account balance would be worth today, which enables Irene to compare what her future savings will buy her based on today's lifestyle costs.

Irene is gobsmacked by this information. She can expect to have **$122 000** in today's dollars for effectively doing nothing—simply for turning up for work. Turning up for work is the start of a great retirement plan.

Table 5.2: Irene banks on 15 more years of super guarantee payments

Super account balance (in today's dollars) at		Delivers annual retirement income (in today's dollars) of	
Start of 15-year period $	End of 15 years $	Until age 87 $	Until age 100 $
Nil	**60 000**	23 000	21 000
20 000	**96 000**	25 000	23 000
35 000	**122 000**	27 000	24 000

Note: Calculations were made using the ASIC MoneySmart superannuation and retirement planner calculators. Annual retirement incomes include the Age Pension and are rounded to the closest thousand dollars (see appendix for table assumptions).

Doing nothing: what will $122 000 in today's dollars give Irene in terms of an annual income and Age Pension?

Based on table 5.1 (see p. 68), Irene will need **$55 000** as a lump sum on retirement (in today's dollars) to live a modest lifestyle (**$21 132** a year) until the age of 100, while also receiving the full Age Pension.

Using the ASIC MoneySmart retirement planner calculator, Irene's **$122 000** lump sum can deliver her an annual retirement income (in today's dollars) of about **$27 000** until the age of 87, or about **$24 000** until the age of 100, including a full Age Pension (see table 5.2). By just turning up for work, Irene can expect to enjoy a lifestyle in retirement that is well beyond modest and more than half-way to a comfortable lifestyle.

What if Irene had started with no superannuation savings at age 52?

If Irene had no superannuation savings today but turned up for work for the next 15 years (see table 5.2), she could expect to have **$60 000** in today's dollars (**$78 000** in tomorrow's dollars). A **$60 000** super account balance on retirement could deliver Irene an annual retirement income (in today's dollars) of about **$23 000** until the age of 87, or about **$21 000** until the age of 100, including the full Age Pension.

Step 6: Take action if a gap exists between how much you want, and what your super and non-super savings are going to deliver

Irene is very excited about her financial position. She had no idea that she would be able to enjoy a lifestyle considerably better than living solely on the Age Pension, right up to age 100, without taking any deliberate action. Irene is now motivated to improve her expected retirement lifestyle.

Usually, Irene has very little spare cash to devote to retirement savings, but since she has now paid off her mortgage she has a spare **$200** a week that she can potentially redirect to her super account. Irene wants to buy a new car in the next few months and believes she needs half of the $200 a week for the deposit on the car and the personal loan repayments.

Irene decides that she can make superannuation contributions of **$100** each week — **$5200** a year. If Irene makes non-concessional (after-tax) contributions to her super fund, she will also be eligible for the co-contribution — a tax-free super contribution from the government of up to **$1000** a year (see chapter 10 for more information).

Aiming for Irene's current after-tax working income of $33 750 a year

Irene uses the ASIC MoneySmart superannuation calculator and discovers that by turning up for work and making additional super contributions of $100 a week, she will have **$238 000** (in today's dollars) when she retires at age 67. That amount can deliver her a retirement income of around **$33 500** in today's dollars until she reaches age 87 (including a substantial part Age Pension), and from age 88 she can expect to rely solely on the Age Pension (see table 5.3).

Irene is amazed that she can create a retirement income of **$33 500** a year (in today's dollars) that delivers her about the same after-tax income that she enjoys now (**$33 750**, for the 2011–12 year). Her expected retirement income can deliver Irene a lifestyle that is substantially more than modest, and very close to a confortable lifestyle, based on the Retirement Standard.

Table 5.3: Irene contributes an extra $100 a week to her super fund and creates a familiar lifestyle in one easy step

Super account balance (in today's dollars) at		Delivers annual retirement income (in today's dollars) of	
Start of 15-year period $	End of 15 years $	Until age 87 $	Until age 100 $
Nil	176 000	30 500	28 000
20 000	212 000	32 500	29 000
35 000	238 000	33 500	30 000

Note: Calculations were made using the ASIC MoneySmart superannuation and retirement planner calculators. Annual retirement incomes include the Age Pension, and are rounded to the closest $500. See the appendix for table assumptions.

Opting for a target income of $31 200 a year (80 per cent of Irene's current before-tax salary)

Irene is a little bit nervous about running out of superannuation money when she reaches the age of 87 and relying solely on the Age Pension, especially if she has to spend money on unexpected costs.

If Irene instead opts for a lower retirement income of **$30 000** (including substantial part Age Pension) from the start of her retirement, she can ensure her savings will last until she reaches age 100 (see table 5.3 on p. 71). Table 5.3 also shows the level of retirement income that Irene could enjoy in retirement even if she started with an account balance of nil or $20 000.

Aiming for a **$30 000** a year income in today's dollars brings Irene's retirement income closer to another possible retirement target — 80 per cent of her current pre-tax salary (**$31 200** — see table 5.1 on p. 68).

Irene realises that she can make a huge difference to her retirement lifestyle by taking a relatively small step now. She starts to believe that she can achieve an even better lifestyle in retirement than she enjoys now — a lot better!

Chasing a more comfortable lifestyle

Irene can hardly believe that her retirement worries can disappear so quickly by simply conducting the Six-Step Wealth Check and running a few numbers through a free, online calculator.

Irene is so pleased with the results of her calculations so far that she decides that she can rev up her retirement plans a bit further. Once she has paid off her new car in five years' time, Irene plans to redirect the other $100 a week used for the loan repayments to her superannuation account. What this means is that:

- for the first five years, Irene will make non-concessional (after-tax) superannuation contributions of **$100** a week (in addition to her employer's compulsory super contributions)

- for the following 10 years to retirement, Irene will contribute **$200** a week to her super account (in addition to her employer's compulsory super contributions)

- for the 15-year period, Irene's employer must make super contributions to her account, according to the SG rules.

If Irene chooses this strategy, she is likely to have **$303 000** in her super account in today's dollars, and have a tax-free retirement income of around **$37 000** a year (including substantial part Age Pension) until the age of 87 — a much better after-tax income than she is enjoying now (see table 5.4).

Irene is very excited. She doesn't believe that it will cost her as much to live in retirement as it does now, so she is already thinking about the comfortable life that she's going to enjoy in retirement — Irene's even planning to start a contingency savings account to give her a financial buffer if she has unexpected health costs or house repairs, or if she wants to take a trip overseas.

Irene is also willing to accept an annual income less than **$37 000** if it means that she has higher income after the age of 87. If Irene accepts an annual retirement income of **$32 000**, her superannuation savings should last until the age of 100 (see table 5.4).

With only a little bit of planning and very little change to her current lifestyle, Irene is now much more relaxed about her financial future. What she finds most amazing is that she now believes that she is able to achieve a similar lifestyle, if not a better lifestyle, to the one she enjoys now.

Table 5.4: Irene contributes an extra $100 a week for five years, then $200 a week for 10 years to create a comfortable lifestyle

Super account balance (in today's dollars) at		Delivers annual retirement income (in today's dollars) of	
Start of 15-year period $	End of 15 years $	Until age 87 $	Until age 100 $
Nil	241 000	34 000	30 000
$20 000	276 000	35 500	31 000
$35 000	303 000	37 000	32 000

Note: Calculations were made using the ASIC MoneySmart superannuation and retirement planner calculators. Annual retirement incomes include the Age Pension, and are rounded to the closest $500. See the appendix for table assumptions.

Part II

You're on your way to
a super plan

Chapter 6

A short course in super: the basics and the best bits

" I think it is really important that you engage energetically
in your learning...but...I think you need time to daydream,
to let your imagination take you where it can. "

Dr Elizabeth Blackburn, 2009 Nobel Prize winner for physiology/medicine

This is the chapter where it's all supposed to happen — the secrets of superannuation wealth unveiled that unlocks the door that leads you to financial freedom.

According to some experts in the superannuation industry, getting Australians interested in superannuation and wealth accumulation is solved by merely telling them about the super rules. If you know the rules, then you're informed and ready for action. Go on, get on with it!

Not really. The super rules are merely a means to an end — the end hopefully being a comfortable life in retirement. What can transform your life after you finish work is this: understanding *how* the super rules can help you create a secure financial future.

Why does superannuation exist?

Superannuation or, more specifically, a superannuation fund, is simply a savings and investment vehicle designed for your retirement. You don't have to save for your retirement using super, but for most Australians, accumulating wealth through a super fund is the most tax-effective way to save for retirement, due to the government offering a cocktail of tax incentives.

If you're an employee, then you don't have a choice about whether you save for retirement via a super fund — your employer is already contributing money to a super fund on your behalf.

Your employer's compulsory contributions are a huge part of the Australian government's grand plan for your retirement, but they are only part of what the government has in mind for your retirement savings plans. The government also wants you to make voluntary super contributions, or accumulate savings outside of superannuation, to bolster your wealth for your retirement. In fact, the government wants you to save for your retirement so much that they offer:

- tax breaks on some super contributions

- a flat rate of tax on super fund earnings

- a tax-free super retirement if you wait until at the least the age of 60 years to retire.

I explain some terms and conditions that apply to the tax incentives in superannuation in the next section.

Tip

The Age Pension remains an important part of the retirement plans for most Australians, especially for women. In most cases, a woman retiring today, or in the future, will be living off a combination of Age Pension and income from superannuation and non-super savings. Based on current statistics, around 80 per cent of retirees will receive a full or part Age Pension when they retire, which means only 20 per cent or so of retirees won't receive any Age Pension at all. This exclusion from the Age Pension is due to the amount of assets they own, or the income they receive from their investments (see chapter 11 for more information on the Age Pension).

How the super world works

The Australian superannuation world is vast — roughly $1.5 trillion dollars is invested in different assets through super funds, on behalf of millions of Australians. Two-thirds of all of this super money is held in fewer than 400 super funds (run by superannuation trustees — see table 6.1), and a support cast of thousands of people helps those super funds invest your money (fund managers), process the paperwork (administrators), look after the actual assets (custodians), pay super benefits (administrators), promote the super fund (in-house marketing team or external consultants), and the list goes on.

Table 6.1: types and number of super funds

Types of fund	Corporate	Industry	Retail	Public sector	Subtotal	SMSFs	Small APRA funds	Total
Numbers	146	61	143	39	389	447620	3521	451530

Source: Extracted from Australian Prudential Regulation Authority, *Statistics, Quarterly Superannuation Performance, March 2011* (issued 9 June 2011).

The other one-third of all super money is invested through more than 400 000 do-it-yourself (DIY) super funds, which are officially known as self managed super funds (SMSFs). DIY super funds can have no more than four members, although typically, they have two members. A small amount of money is invested through another type of small super fund, run on behalf of members by professional trustees — known as a small APRA fund. APRA stands for the Australian Prudential Regulation Authority, the main super regulator.

I have quoted you some big numbers, but the key number you need to remember is five. If you're trying to understand how the super world works, it may help to know that there are only five types of super funds in Australia — four different large super funds, and then small super funds:

- *Industry super funds.* An industry fund can cater for workers from a particular industry, although many of them are now available to anyone.

- *Retail super funds or master trusts.* Retail funds are run by financial institutions, including banks, financial planning groups and fund managers. If you visit a financial adviser you may also hear the terms wrap, platform and master trust — all of which offer you access to a lot of managed funds, rather than a single super fund.

- *Company (or corporate) super funds.* Generally speaking, only employees working for the company can join the company super fund. Some company funds do permit relatives of existing members to join.

- *Public sector super funds.* These are available only to public sector employees and, in some cases, ex-public sector employees — where an employee leaves the public service but can remain a member of the super fund.

- *Small super funds (self managed super funds or small APRA funds).* Even though there are two types of small funds — self managed super funds (SMSFs, or DIY funds) and small APRA funds — those Aussies keen to take total control of their super generally opt for an SMSF.

Tip

Generally speaking, you can choose from only three types of super-annuation funds: industry funds, retail funds or small super funds. If you're already a member of a company super fund, or a public sector fund, then you usually can remain a fund member of this type of super fund, but corporate and public sector super funds are usually not open to the general public. (See tip 7 on p. 159 for information on choosing a super fund.)

Do you know which type of super fund you belong to? I provide a lot more information on the different types of super funds on my free consumer website, SuperGuide at <www.superguide.com.au>.

Top 10 super rules, at your service

Try a simple exercise. I'll provide a short list of the main rules on superannuation, and you can take a few moments to mull over what that list has prompted you to think about, and perhaps motivated you to do, in terms of saving for retirement. Here are my top 10 super rules:

1 *Superannuation guarantee (SG).* Your employer must contribute money to your member account in a super fund on your behalf. This obligation is imposed on employers under the SG laws. Compulsory employer contributions are often called SG contributions.

2 *Tax on concessional (before-tax) contributions.* Your employer's compulsory SG contributions and any before-tax contributions that you choose to make (known as concessional contributions) are taxed at a maximum rate of 15 per cent when the super contributions enter the super fund. In comparison, a woman earning $37 000 a year or more can expect to pay at least 30 per cent income tax (for 2011–12, or at least 32.5 per cent for 2012–13, subject to the legislation being passed) on that same income (and up to 45 per cent if she earns more than $180 000), when she chooses not to make before-tax super contributions.

3 *Special tax rate on investment earnings.* Earnings on your super fund's investments are also taxed at no more than 15 per cent.

4 *Co-contribution.* If you make non-concessional (after-tax) contributions to your super fund, depending on your level of income, the government may put some tax-free money into your super fund for you. This is known as the co-contribution.

5 *Contributions caps.* The amount of super contributions that you can make each year is capped, unless you are happy paying extra tax. If you make super contributions that exceed the caps you will have to pay penalty tax.

6 *Fund choice.* In many cases you can choose the super fund you want your employer's SG contributions paid into. If you don't choose your super fund, your employer chooses for you. In certain instances, your super fund may be determined by an employment agreement or industrial award.

7 *Investment choice.* In most cases you can decide how you want your money invested by the super fund by choosing from your super fund's investment options. If you don't make an investment choice, then your super money is invested in a default investment option. The default option is typically invested in a range of assets, known as a balanced investment option. Investments are spread across higher risk and lower risk assets as a means of maximising investment returns while managing the risk that some investments may lose money.

Top 10 super rules, at your service (cont'd)

8 *Member reporting.* Your super fund must send you regular reports (at least annually) on the fund's performance, and on your own super account's performance. Your super fund must also state fees charged, and show you any other transactions on your super account (such as the deductions for insurance premiums and taxes).

9 *Preservation.* Your money is preserved in super. That means you generally can't take your money (your benefits) out of the super fund until you retire at or after your preservation age (from age 55 to 60, depending on your date of birth), or when you satisfy another condition of release. To be allowed to withdraw your super you must, in super's technical language, satisfy a condition of release and these conditions are very specific (see chapter 11 for more information).

10 *Tax-free for over sixties.* When you retire on after the age of 60, you pay no tax on your superannuation benefits, unless you're a long-term public servant. And there's more! When you receive a pension (which super funds may also call an income stream) from your super fund, the earnings on the assets that finance your pension are also exempt from tax, even when you retire before the age of 60 (see chapter 11 for information on the tax treatment of super benefits).

Are you excited yet? No? What about the rule delivering tax-free super for over sixties? Maybe you vagued out by the time you reached that fascinating and alluring superannuation rule. Merely stating the super rules on websites (not mine of course), or in brochures encouraging financial literacy, or in some books is why this important topic has been unfairly tagged with the title *boring*.

A key question to ask is this: how can the top 10 super rules help me create a worry-free financial future?

And here's what the super rules can do for you

It's important to appreciate the possibilities of what you can do with the super rules. How do they apply to your situation and how will they help give you a better life in retirement? One possible response to this question could be this: saving and investing in superannuation can be the most effective way for me to accumulate wealth for retirement for the following reasons:

- Compulsory, regular contributions paid by my employer mean that someone is doing the saving for me.

- Compound earnings (see chapter 3) mean that I'm earning investment returns on my super account's reinvested returns, which grows my savings faster.

- Tax concessions on super fund earnings also help my super account to grow even faster, because more savings are retained in my super account.

- Tax incentives linked to super contributions (see later in chapter) mean that I can save more for retirement, while reducing my income tax bill.

- No tax on the earnings of my super pension assets means that my retirement money will last longer when I do eventually retire.

Superannuation guarantee is a great start

Superannuation guarantee (SG) is the official description for your employer's compulsory superannuation contributions. The law currently requires your employer to pay the equivalent of 9 per cent of your wages or salary from your ordinary hours of work as super contributions, when you earn more than $450 a month. For example, if you earn $50 000 a year, then your employer contributes $4500 to your super fund each year, usually in quarterly or monthly payments. If you earn $30 000 a year, then your employer contributes $2700 a year. If you earn $60 000 a year, your employer contributes $5400 a year to your superannuation fund.

In time, your employer will have to contribute more to your super account under the SG rules, which should generate bigger retirement payouts because you will have more money invested for your retirement. Subject to the legislation being passed, from July 2013 the SG percentage will gradually increase from 9 per cent until it reaches 12 per cent from July 2019 onwards (see table 6.2, overleaf).

Who is eligible for SG?

You're eligible for SG contributions from your employer when you earn a minimum of $450 a month, and you're under the age of 70. Some people may work under an award that requires an employer to make super contributions even when the employee earns less than $450 a month.

Table 6.2: how much super must my employer contribute under the SG rules?

From start of financial year	Rate %
2011–12	9.00
2012–13	9.00
2013–14	9.25
2014–15	9.50
2015–16	10.00
2016–17	10.50
2017–18	11.00
2018–19	11.50
2019–20	12.00

Source: Adapted from table in Australian government fact sheet 'Superannuation—Increasing the Superannuation Guarantee rate to 12 per cent', on the Stronger, Fairer, Simpler website at <www.futuretax.gov.au>. In mid 2011, the legislation introducing the SG increase (effective from July 2013) had not yet been passed.

Tip

Your ordinary hours of work include over-award payments, shift or casual loading, performance bonuses or commissions. Your employer doesn't have to pay SG on any overtime you work, and if you have a salary package that includes, say, a car or additional before-tax super contributions, your employer is only required to pay 9 per cent on the cash component of your salary. In some cases an employer will continue to pay 9 per cent SG based on a person's total salary, rather than just the cash component, but this approach will depend on the arrangement the employee has negotiated with her employer.

Special rules apply for individuals employed in domestic or private work, or if an employee is under the age of 18. If you're employed for domestic or private work, such as babysitting, gardening or cleaning, you must work more than 30 hours a week and earn a minimum of $450 a month before your employer has to make SG contributions. If you're under 18, you also have to work more than 30 hours a week and earn a minimum of $450 per month to be eligible for SG.

> ## Tip
>
> There is a dollar limit to what your employer must pay in SG contributions. If you earn more than $175 280 for the 2011–12 financial year—lucky you—then your employer is only required to pay 9 per cent of $175 280, as if you had this level of income, even when you earn more than this impressive amount. If you're fortunate enough to be in this position, then the most likely scenario is that your employer's compulsory super contributions form part of your overall salary package, rather than paid in addition to your salary (see Lily's story below for an explanation of the difference between *plus* super and *including* super).

> ## Tip
>
> From July 2013, SG will be extended to employees aged 70 to 74, subject to legislation being passed.

Lily's story: plus super is better than including super

Lily is 55 and works part time as a senior manager in administration for a major public hospital. She has always worked part time, but often sporadically. Only recently has she been able to commit to such a full-on job now that the demands of looking after her four children have eased. Lily earns **$50 000** a year *plus* super. Lily's SG entitlement is 9 per cent of $50 000, which works out at **$4500** a year. Her SG entitlement takes her total pay to **$54 500** (see table 6.3, overleaf).

Lily's friend, Milijan, is employed in a similar part-time role in a private hospital but he receives **$50 000** a year *including* super, from his employer. Milijan assumes he is on a similar package to Lily but the term *including* means different SG entitlements, and a big difference in total pay. Milijan's $50 000 a year package means that he receives **$45 782** in salary plus **$4128** in SG. Lily's package is worth **$4500** more than Milijan's package ($4218 more in salary, and $372 more in SG—see table 6.3).

Table 6.3: SG entitlements—plus or including super?

	Lily	Milijan
	$50 000 a year plus super	**$50 000 a year including super**
Salary	$50 000	$45 782
SG	$4 500	$4 128
Total remuneration	**$54 500**	**$50 000**

Tip

In chapter 7, I show you how Lily, at 55 years of age, can turn her $4500 a year in SG contributions into a $300 000 retirement balance.

No harm in checking up on your employer

A popular question that I receive on my website, SuperGuide at <www.superguide.com.au> is: How do I check that my employer is paying my SG entitlement into my super fund?

Your employer must pay your quarterly SG entitlements within 28 days of the end of each three months (see table 6.4), although your employer may be paying SG contributions monthly or fortnightly. You can check that your employer is paying your SG contributions in the following way:

1 Check that the payment date for your quarterly SG contribution has passed.

2 Check with your super fund that the SG contribution has reached your super account, after allowing a few days for your super fund to process the contribution. You may be able to find this information online. Many super funds offer fund members special access to account information through the super fund's website. You can also phone your super fund and ask for this information. If your super fund has no record of your employer's SG contribution then you may need to approach your employer.

3 Ask your employer or pay officer if, and when, the SG contribution was made.

4 Hopefully, your employer has paid your SG contribution. If not, or you are fairly certain that your employer hasn't paid, then you can contact the Australian Tax Office Superannuation Hotline on 13 10 20 and request that the ATO investigate your circumstances.

Table 6.4: employer deadlines for payment of SG

Payment period	SG deadline for each three-month period
1 July – 30 September	28 October
1 October – 31 December	28 January
1 January – 31 March	28 April
1 April – 30 June	28 July

Good news alert no. 5: looking for an easy way to make $300 000?

Turning $4500 into a $300 000 lump sum may sound fanciful but it's possible, just by turning up for work. You can be 25, 35, 45, 55, or older, and have a healthy nest egg for your retirement by getting on with life. Want to know the super secret? I'll give you a tip: your employer's SG contributions have a lot to do with it. In chapter 7, I share the stories of four women who turned $4500 in SG contributions into $300 000 the easy way.

Your own contributions and all that jazz

You can also add your own money to your super account, in the form of voluntary superannuation contributions. You can make two types of voluntary super contributions — non-concessional and concessional contributions. They sound the same, which can be confusing, but the two types of super contributions are quite different.

The next few sections of this chapter contain some important but technical terms, which can make for tiring reading. Now might be a good time to take a five-minute breather and make yourself a cuppa!

Non-concessional (after-tax) contributions

You make a non-concessional contribution from your after-tax income, or after-tax savings. For example, you can make regular or one-off payments to your super fund from your personal bank account, or you can make one-off contributions when you receive financial windfalls, such as a tax refund, an inheritance or after-tax proceeds from a property sale.

Under the super rules, when a non-concessional (after-tax) contribution is paid into a super fund, the fund does not deduct tax from that contribution. Note, however, that any earnings your fund receives from investing these contributions will then form part of your super account's earnings, and be subject to earnings tax (at a tax rate of 15 per cent).

Concessional (before-tax) contributions

Any superannuation contribution where an individual or company receives a tax deduction or tax concession for making the payment is called a concessional contribution. Concessional contributions are made from before-tax income. The super fund has to pay 15 per cent contributions tax on the concessional contribution (which is deducted from your super account), although if you earn more than $37 000 a year, that's a lot less tax than you are paying on your income (see the appendix for income tax rates).

Any super contributions that you make as part of a salary sacrifice arrangement with your employer, or that you claim as a tax deduction if you are self-employed, are treated as concessional contributions (see chapters 9 and 10 for more information).

Your employer's compulsory SG contributions are treated as concessional contributions because your employer gets a tax deduction for making these contributions on your behalf.

Super contributions — other interesting tidbits

If you're considering making your own superannuation contributions, then find out as much as you can about the contribution rules, and the conditions that your super fund may place on how such contributions can be paid (for example, check whether your super fund offers or requires payment by direct debit rather than cheque), and what application form you need to complete and submit to your super fund.

More important facts about super contributions include:

- *Tax-free bonus super contribution — co-contribution.* If you choose to make non-concessional (after-tax) contributions, then you may be eligible for a tax-free bonus contribution from the government called the super co-contribution. If your income is below a certain level, and you make a non-concessional contribution, then the government will give you money direct to your super fund (see tip 13 on p. 169). You don't even have to apply for it. Not bad.

- *Work test for over 65s.* Even when you're not working, you can make superannuation contributions until you reach the age of 65. If you're aged 65 or over, however, you must meet a work test before you can make a super contribution. The work test is not particularly onerous — you must work for 40 hours in a 30-day period at some time during a financial year (1 July to following 30 June) to be able to contribute to a super fund in that financial year. After you reach the age of 75, you can no longer make super contributions.

- *Watch the contributions caps.* The government encourages you to make super contributions, but only up to a limit. There are annual caps for both concessional and non-concessional contributions. If you exceed the contributions caps, then you will have to pay penalty tax (which is usually deducted from your super account). Yuk! (See chapter 10 for more information.)

Super delivers a triple bonus in tax savings

If it were not for the tax incentives, a superannuation account could easily be like any other managed fund or even savings account. Superannuation exists because of the tax incentives available, and those incentives operate at three main stages:

- when you or your employer make super contributions

- when your super fund makes money on investments on your behalf

- when your super fund pays you a pension or a lump sum.

Potentially lower tax through super contributions

If you make a concessional (before-tax) contribution, then the maximum tax that you will pay on that contribution is 15 per cent. If you pay more than 15 per cent income tax on your personal income (see the appendix for income tax rates), then making voluntary concessional contributions can save you tax (be tax-effective). If you chose not to make the contribution, then you could be paying up to 45 per cent tax (plus the Medicare levy) on that money, depending on how much income you earn. If you pay less than 15 per cent in income tax then check out the box 'Pssst! Super's not fair for everyone' on this page.

When your employer makes a concessional SG contribution on your behalf, the employer claims a tax deduction, and your super fund deducts 15 per cent tax from your super contribution.

Psst! Super's not fair for everyone

If you pay 15 per cent or less in income tax on your regular income, then superannuation is not that exciting from a tax point of view when you are saving for retirement. Anyone earning less than $37 000 (for 2011–12 or, from 2012–13, anyone earning less than $18 200, or $20 542 when you take into account the low income tax offset, subject to the legislation being passed), receives no real income tax benefit from saving and investing through a superannuation fund. As a super fund member, your fund pays 15 per cent tax on earnings, and if you choose to make concessional (before-tax) contributions, then your super contributions are subject to 15 per cent tax as well.

Now, that doesn't seem fair, especially when your employer is required to make super contributions on your behalf.

The Australian government agrees and it has plans to introduce a tax rebate system to refund the super tax paid on the super contributions of Australians who pay more tax on super contributions than they pay in income tax (not yet law). From July 2012, if you pay less than 15 per cent tax on your adjusted taxable income, and your employer makes concessional (before-tax) superannuation contributions on your behalf, then you can expect the contributions tax that has been deducted from your super account to be refunded to your super account.

For example, if you earn $30 000 as an employee, your employer must currently pay the equivalent of 9 per cent of the $30 000, that is, $2700, as quarterly SG contributions. Contributions tax of $405 is payable on the SG contributions, and the Australian government will refund this tax to your super account, in the following financial year, after you lodge your tax return for that year.

For individuals paying less than 15 per cent tax on their personal income, making non-concessional (after-tax) contributions may be a useful strategy in certain circumstances. If you make a non-concessional contribution and satisfy an income test, the government will pay up to $1000 into your super account. This payment is called a co-contribution. The co-contribution is a cash bonus, and it's tax-free! (See chapter 10 for more information.)

Lower tax on investment income

A super fund must pay tax on investment earnings, just like you and I have to pay tax when we earn money. The maximum tax on super fund earnings, however, is 15 per cent, unlike the potential maximum for individuals of 45 per cent (plus the Medicare levy).

The higher the income that you earn outside super, the more tax-effective superannuation becomes, because instead of paying 30, 37 or 45 per cent on investment earnings outside super (for 2011–12, and 19, 32.5, 37 or 45 per cent in 2012–13, subject to the legislation being passed), you pay a maximum of 15 per cent on investment earnings within super. If you pay more than 15 per cent tax on your non-super income, you may then be able to accumulate wealth much faster in a super fund because you are giving less money to the tax man.

Tax-free super benefits on retirement

If you retire on or after age 60, you can withdraw your benefits free of tax — that's a tax-free retirement. If you retire before the age of 60, then some tax may be payable on your retirement benefits. If you take a superannuation pension before or after the age of 60, then you can benefit from another tax-free super feature — no tax on fund earnings. When your super fund invests the money from your pension account, you pay no tax on the fund earnings from the investments sourced from your pension account money. You can enjoy tax-free benefits (except for some public servants), and tax-free earnings on pension assets. I explain what happens when you retire in more detail in chapter 11, including the special tax treatment of super benefits paid to some public servants.

How does your super fund invest your money?

The key to understanding how superannuation works and how your super fund invests your super savings is appreciating that a superannuation fund is not an investment. A superannuation fund is an investor, just like you and I can be investors.

You may be thinking: what's the difference, and does it matter?

Yes, it does matter because many Australians, including journalists, seem to think that superannuation is either a good or a bad investment, when a superannuation fund is merely a vehicle for investment. A superannuation fund can invest in shares, property, cash or other assets, just like any other investor. For example, consider how two different funds invest. The Ultra Conservative Super fund invests all of its money in term deposits (also known as a cash investment), while the Eager to Grow Super fund invests all of its money in Australian shares. If interest rates increase, the Ultra Conservative Super Fund will perform well. If the prices of shares and company dividends increase, then the Eager to Grow super fund will perform strongly.

Diversification can help manage risk

A superannuation fund is run by trustees who invest your super money on your behalf. Typically, they appoint asset consultants who work out the appropriate balance of higher risk assets (such as shares and property) and lower risk assets (such as cash and fixed interest) for the super fund, or for the specific investment options available from the super fund. This process is called asset allocation.

Super fund trustees invariably appoint investment managers (or employ investment experts) to select specific investments for the investment options, which should then reflect the asset allocation decided by the super trustees.

Diversification, that is, putting money into more than one investment, or investing in more than one type of asset (such as shares, property and cash), can help your super account deliver decent returns while attempting to smooth some of the bumpier years, when riskier assets, such as shares, might be performing badly.

Your super fund's long-term investment performance is determined by the quality of the underlying investments that your super fund holds. What seems to confuse most people is asset allocation — *how* a super fund allocates money to the different asset classes — such as shares, property and cash.

Asset allocation matters

Most Australians have their super money invested in their super fund's balanced or growth investment options. In these investment options, between 60 and 80 per cent of their super money is invested in shares, property and other higher risk assets (which also earn higher returns when they are doing well), while between 20 and 40 per cent of their super money is invested in more conservative investments, such as cash and other income-producing assets, such as government bonds. Conservative, or income-style, investments are lower risk, because they are less likely to experience losses than growth assets (such as shares), but over the longer term they deliver lower returns than the higher risk assets.

What does this type of asset allocation — balanced or growth — mean for your retirement savings? A balanced or growth investment portfolio (which has a larger allocation to higher risk investments) can lead to higher long-term returns than more conservative investment options, although you should also note the following:

- Over the longer term, shares and property deliver higher returns, but they can have shocking years as well.

- Since most Australians have a fair bit of their super invested in higher risk assets, such as shares and property, when the share market falls at the same time as the listed property market plummets, as it did in 2008 and 2009 (this period is now known as the global financial crisis, or GFC), everyone's super accounts suffer as well.

- When the Australian share market began to recover during 2010 and 2011, the returns on most superannuation accounts improved as well, because of the relatively high allocation to Australian shares in most super funds.

Tip

If you had chosen your own investment option within your super fund, and you had chosen a cash option before and during the global financial crisis, your super account is unlikely to have suffered any losses at all. The lesson from this comparison is not necessarily to have all of your super money in cash, or to invest all of your super money in shares or property, but to understand how the risk and return associated with an asset class or a specific investment can help you work out the risk you're willing to take when accumulating savings for your retirement. I explore the investment options available within super funds in chapter 10 (tips 8 and 9 on p. 160–162), and how investing works in chapter 3.

Tip

Each year, your super fund must, by law, provide you with a full report on how your super account has performed, and where your super money is invested. I recommend that you read this document. If you can't find your latest report (most super funds send out reports around September–October each year), contact your super fund for another copy, or download it from your super fund's website. Many super funds provide updates more often than once a year.

Good news alert no. 6: lower fees can mean 20 per cent more in super

In a fancy document called a product disclosure statement (PDS), your super fund must warn you that small differences in investment performance and fees can have a huge impact on your super account's long-term returns. For example, if you pay total annual fees of 2 per cent of your account balance, rather than, say, 1 per cent of your account balance each year, then over a 30-year period you will end up with a 20 per cent smaller final balance in your super account.

In other words, you could end up with $160 000 rather than $200 000. Or, you could end up with $320 000 rather than $400 000. Ouch!

Higher fees can mean a smaller retirement balance, but so can lower investment returns. Likewise, a 1 per cent difference in investment returns over a 30-year period can also mean a 20 per cent difference in your final account balance. (See tip 7 on p. 159 for more information on choosing a fund if you're unhappy with your super fund's fees or investment returns, and tips 8 and 9 on p. 160–162 for information on changing your investment option.)

Chapter 7

Doing a little: turn $4500 into $300000 the easy way

> " When you make a world tolerable for yourself, you make a world tolerable for others. "
>
> *Anäis Nin, author and diarist*

You have many options when you start thinking about building wealth for retirement. You can decide to do nothing about your financial future, or you can do a little, or you can do a lot.

Even when you think you're doing nothing, there's a good chance you're already doing something productive towards your retirement. If you have a job, turning up for work means that you're automatically accumulating wealth for your retirement. Your employer, by law, is required to deposit money into your super account, at least every three months, each year of your working life.

If you have had a job in the past, then any compulsory employer contributions (made under the SG laws), plus earnings on those original contributions, are also accumulating for your eventual retirement. Not a bad start to your retirement plan!

It's possible for anyone to convert employer superannuation contributions into a significant lump sum over time, just by turning up for work. For example, you can be any age — 25, 35, 45 or 55 — and turn $4500 of SG contributions into $300000 or more (based on an annual income of $50000). If you're willing to kick in a few super contributions of your own, your $4500 starting point could potentially become $500000 or more.

In this chapter, I provide four case studies to show how steps 4, 5 and 6 of my Six-Step Wealth Check (see chapter 4) can operate, and to show you how easy it can be for you to improve your financial circumstances for retirement.

If you are self-employed

If you are self-employed, you won't have access to the SG system, unless you run your business as a company. If you have a company structure in place then you *must* make super contributions on behalf of each of your company's employees, including yourself. In this case, you should find the case studies in this chapter very useful.

If you don't run your business under a company structure, then you need to make a special effort to save for your retirement. The case studies in this chapter are still useful if you don't have an employer. You can make tax-deductible super contributions (see chapter 10) that match what an employer would contribute. For example, in the doing nothing scenarios (SG only), you can replace the employer contribution with your own $4500 tax-deductible super contribution (based on the SG entitlement for a person on an annual income of $50 000).

You can check out the case studies in this chapter to get a feel for how you can build your super benefit over time. You can also head to chapters 8 and 9, where I explore the options for those women who have to be, or choose to be, more proactive when saving for retirement. But remember, if you have been an employee at any time since 1992 (and for some employees since the mid 1980s), then you're likely to have a super account quietly growing on your behalf, courtesy of your previous employer's compulsory super contributions.

How four women turned $4500 into $300 000 the easy way

Four women, ranging in age from 25 to 55, discovered they can look forward to a reasonable standard of living in retirement simply by turning up for work each day, and doing a little bit of retirement planning. Let me introduce you to the four women:

- Chrissy, age 25, currently has no super (case study 1 on p. 100)

- Julie, age 35, has $15 000 in super (case study 2 on p. 103)

- Sahn, age 45, has $35 000 in super (case study 3 on p. 106)

- Lily, age 55, has $70 000 in super (case study 4 on p. 109).

The four case studies consider four key points for each of the women:

- how much super they have today (step 4 of my Six-Step Wealth Check)

- how much super they will have when they retire if they keep doing what they are currently doing (step 5 of my Six-Step Wealth Check)

- some simple steps they can take to boost their final superannuation balance (step 6 of my Six-Step Wealth Check)

- how the different super strategies affect the level of retirement income.

For simplicity, throughout the case studies, I assume that SG remains at 9 per cent of each woman's salary, even though the government intends to increase the SG rate from July 2013 until it reaches 12 per cent from July 2019 (when legislation is passed). What this means is that the actual final retirement payout for each woman should be slightly higher than the amounts discussed in the case studies.

Tip

Each of the women in the four case studies earns $50 000 a year. If you earn less than $50 000, then the case studies can still be very helpful. You can replace the $50 000 with any level of income you choose, and you can then use the free website calculators that I refer to throughout this chapter to make the calculations for yourself. I explain how you can use the calculators, and I list all of the assumptions used in the case studies, in the appendix.

The four women in the case studies make voluntary super contributions as a way of boosting their super. I use non-concessional contributions, that is, super contributions sourced from after-tax income, to illustrate how easy it can be to boost your final retirement balance. Non-concessional contributions are not the only type of voluntary super contribution that you can make. If you pay more than 15 cents tax in the dollar — anyone earning more than $37 000 in the 2011–12 financial year falls into this category (or from 2012–13, anyone earning more than $18 200, or $20 542 when you take into account the low income tax offset, subject to the legislation being passed) — then concessional (before-tax) contributions may be a tax-effective way to save for your retirement.

Ten handy facts about your superannuation guarantee entitlements

The four case studies in this chapter assume that the women involved receive compulsory contributions from an employer under the SG laws. Here is a list of the most important SG facts you need to know (check out chapter 6 for a more detailed explanation of how SG works):

1 Your employer must make super contributions, at least quarterly, based on an annual entitlement of 9 per cent of your ordinary earnings. From July 2013, the required percentage increases to 9.25 per cent, and will gradually increase to 12 per cent by July 2019 (subject to the legislation being passed).

2 You must earn at least $450 a month to be eligible for SG.

3 If you do private or domestic work, such as babysitting, gardening or cleaning, then you must work at least 30 hours, and earn at least $450 a month to be eligible for SG.

4 If you're less than 18 years old, then you must work at least 30 hours and earn at least $450 a month to be eligible for SG.

5 If you are aged 70 or over, you are not entitled to SG until the 2013–14 financial year. From July 2013, eligible individuals aged 70 to 74 will receive SG contributions from employers.

6 Your super entitlement must be paid to your super fund at least every three months. If not paid, you can complain to the Australian Tax Office.

7 If you earn big bucks, then your SG entitlement is subject to a cap, known as the maximum contributions base. For 2011–12, an employer is required to make SG contributions on 9 per cent of salary up to an annual salary limit of $175 280 ($43 820 each quarter).

8 When you start a new job, check whether your pay is $x *plus* super, or $x *including* super, and what that means for your total remuneration package. (See chapter 6 for an explanation of the difference between the two pay options.)

9 Watch out when negotiating salary sacrifice arrangements—your employer could cut your SG. I briefly explain salary sacrifice arrangements in chapters 9 and 10. I analyse the treatment of SG when you salary sacrifice on my free website, SuperGuide at <www.superguide.com.au>.

10 If you're self-employed you may still be eligible for SG in certain circumstances. You can find more information about contractors and SG by phoning the Australian Taxation Office's Superannuation Infoline on 13 10 20, or by visiting the ATO's website at <www.ato.gov.au>. Also, check out the box on p. 96 for tips on how the four case studies in this chapter can help you plan for retirement.

Lump sum amounts, annual retirement incomes and annual salaries quoted in the four case studies in this chapter are in today's dollars. Due to the effects of rising prices (inflation) over time, amounts quoted need to be adjusted back to what your money can buy today to make it easy to compare different lifestyles, or to compare the outcomes of using different superannuation strategies. In this chapter and throughout this book, you will read figures expressed in today's dollars. For example, if you're hoping to live on, say, $40 000 a year when you retire, you need to think about what $40 000 can buy you in 10, 15 or 20 years' time. (See chapter 3 for more information.)

Tip

Annual retirement incomes quoted in this chapter are tax-free incomes. They are sourced from super savings and the Age Pension. If you're aged at least 60 and you retire, you can receive your superannuation benefits tax-free— as a lump sum or as an income stream (with the exception of some public servants—see chapter 11). If you are over Age Pension age, you can generally take advantage of more generous tax rules on non-super income, which means you can expect to pay no tax on the annual retirement incomes quoted in this chapter when your sources of income in retirement are from only your super benefits and the Age Pension.

> ## Tip
>
> In addition to six-monthly adjustments to the Age Pension rates, from July 2012 a person's Age Pension entitlement will include a clean energy supplement (subject to the legislation being passed—see chapter 11 for more information). What this means for Chrissy, Julie, Sahn and Lily is that when the Age Pension adjustments take effect, the four women will need slightly less super to achieve the same annual retirement incomes listed in the following tables and text.

Case study 1 (age 25): Chrissy's counting on a cushy retirement

Chrissy is aged 25 and starts a new job paying $50 000 a year. She currently has no super because she was previously self-employed. Chrissy has watched her grandparents struggle on the Age Pension, and now her parents are struggling because her mother has had to retire early due to ill-health. Her family's experience has motivated Chrissy to start planning for her retirement, even though her friends think she's mad to worry about it at such a young age. The first bit of good news that Chrissy discovers is that her employer will pay $4500 a year into a super fund on her behalf, just for Chrissy turning up for work each day. Chrissy also learns that she is part of the first generation of Australians who will enjoy the benefits of at least 9 per cent SG for her full working life.

Doing nothing delivers Chrissy a massive $400 000 retirement nest egg

Using the MoneySmart superannuation calculator, Chrissy works out that her employer's contributions can give her these retirement balances:

- *If Chrissy works until the age of 65*, that is, for 40 years, and she remains on **$50 000** a year in today's dollars (that is, adjusted for inflation) for her working life, her superannuation account will grow to **$360 000** in today's dollars (see table 7.1 on p. 102). Note that Chrissy will not be able to claim the Age Pension until she turns 67, due to her date of birth.

- *If Chrissy works until the age of 67* (her Age Pension age), her super account will grow to **$396 000**! Chrissy will have close to **$400 000** in her super account just for turning up for work each day (see table 7.1). That's a huge amount from a small start of **$4500**.

Doing a little gives Chrissy $46 000 a year in retirement, from a $500 000 lump sum

If Chrissy contributes, say, 2 per cent of her **$50 000** salary in non-concessional (after-tax) contributions for the same period, that is $1000 each year (about $20 a week) for her working life, she will have **$510 000** when she retires, again just for turning up for work (see table 7.1, overleaf).

By making a non-concessional contribution of $1000, and earning an income less than the upper threshold for receiving the co-contribution, Chrissy is eligible for a small government co-contribution (see chapter 10), which also helps her super savings grow.

Chrissy then uses the MoneySmart retirement planner calculator to estimate what this superannuation balance can deliver in terms of a retirement income. She is astounded to discover that, without doing much at all, she will have a retirement income of 90 per cent of her before-tax working income by the time she turns 67 (Age Pension age): that's around **$46 000** a year in retirement (including part Age Pension), until at least the age of 87, adjusted annually to cover rising prices.

Tip

What Chrissy finds most amazing is that, after she takes into account the tax she pays on her current salary ($8750 for 2011–12), her income in retirement will be much higher than her current after-tax income. For 2011–12, Chrissy's after-tax working income is $41 250, and she can expect to receive a tax-free retirement income of around **$46 000** (including part Age Pension), until the age of 87. If Chrissy aims for a target retirement income that is identical to her current after-tax income of **$41 250** (see the appendix for income tax rates for later years), then she can expect this level of income (including a part Age Pension) to last until the age of 93. Not bad. If she is willing to accept a lower income in retirement, she can receive an income of **$38 230** (including a part Age Pension) and extend her financial freedom until the age of 100!

Chrissy can now get on with living life, with her retirement planning sorted. If she wants a higher income in retirement, she can consider contributing more money later in her working life.

Table 7.1 lists the account balances that Chrissy can expect when she retires at age 67 and does nothing (SG only), and when she makes an annual after-tax contribution of between $1000 (doing a little) and $5000 (doing heaps).

Table 7.1: Chrissy's super balance if she does nothing, a little, heaps or has a work break (age 25, nil starting balance, income $50 000 a year)

Chrissy (from age 25)	Doing nothing (9% SG only)		Making after-tax contributions	Break from work (for 10 years)
Super contributions	Until age 65 $	Until age 67 $	Until age 67 $	Until age 67 $
Doing nothing				
SG only	360 000	396 000	n/a	289 000
Non-concessional (after-tax) contributions				
Doing a little				
SG + $1000 a year	n/a	n/a	510 000	378 000
Doing more				
SG + $2000 a year	n/a	n/a	613 000	453 000
Doing a lot				
SG + $3000 a year	n/a	n/a	717 000	529 000
Doing heaps				
SG + $5000 a year	n/a	n/a	924 000	680 000

Note: See appendix for table assumptions.

What happens if Chrissy has a break from work?

Chrissy expects to take time out of the workforce to have children. She thinks she may be bringing up her children full time for up to 10 years. Using the MoneySmart superannuation calculator (see table 7.1), Chrissy's superannuation balance at age 67 (taking into account the 10-year break from work) will be:

- **$289 000**, when she relies only on SG contributions

- **$378 000**, if she also makes contributions of $1000 a year for the years that she works, that is for 32 years, rather than 42 years (the work break is taken from age 35 to age 45, and during that 10-year period Chrissy earns no income and makes no super contributions).

A retirement balance of **$378 000** can deliver Chrissy an annual income in retirement of about **$40 000** (including a part Age Pension) until the age of 87 — 80 per cent of her current salary and just under her current after-tax income of **$41 250** (for 2011–12; from age 88 Chrissy relies solely on the Age Pension). This amount gives Chrissy a retirement income better than the Retirement Standard's comfortable lifestyle, and considerably more than a comfortable lifestyle if she is part of a couple, because of the Age Pension entitlements available for a couple (see case study 3 on p. 106).

If Chrissy has a break from work, and also wants her savings to last until she reaches the age of 100, then she can expect to live on about **$34 000** a year (including a part Age Pension) when she makes super contributions of $1000 a year while she is working. Chrissy could further increase her super contributions from today, or when she's older.

How much does a modest or comfortable lifestyle cost?

The Retirement Standard measures the cost of a modest or comfortable lifestyle in retirement (see chapter 4 for more information). According to the Retirement Standard, assuming you own your own home, you need the following amounts of money, after tax, to give you a modest or comfortable lifestyle:

- as a single person, you need **$21 132** a year for a modest lifestyle, and **$39 302** a year for a comfortable lifestyle

- as a couple, you need **$30 557** a year for a modest lifestyle and **$53 729** a year for a comfortable lifestyle.

Case study 2 (age 35): Julie's jump in retirement expectations

Chrissy's friend Julie is aged 35. Chrissy tells Julie how excited she is about her super account and how easy it is to accumulate retirement savings when you do a little bit of planning. Although Julie earns the same income as Chrissy — $50 000 a year — she is sceptical about her own financial future because she doesn't plan to be in the workforce for another 40 years. She wants to retire by the time she *is 60, which means she will only receive another 25 years of SG contributions. She only has $15 000 in her super account because she took 10 years off from paid employment to raise her three children.*

Doing nothing: what if Julie relies only on her employer's super contributions?

Julie uses the MoneySmart superannuation calculator and discovers that if she just gets on with life and does nothing with her super, her employer's compulsory contributions (SG) of **$4500** a year will still deliver **$198 000** in today's dollars when she is 60 (see table 7.2).

Retiring early is possible but requires a lot of planning. If Julie retires at 60, rather than 67 (her Age Pension age), she will not receive any Age Pension for the first seven years of her retirement, which means that she must rely only on her superannuation and non-super savings.

Doing a lot and retiring at 60 means Julie has a nest egg of more than $300 000

Julie is surprised with the result for doing nothing but turning up for work, so she uses the MoneySmart superannuation calculator to work out how much super she could have when she finishes work if she makes non-concessional (after-tax) contributions of 6 per cent — **$3000** a year — until the age of 60 (see table 7.2). Julie is relieved that she will have **$329 000** in super by the time she turns 60.

Using the MoneySmart retirement planner calculator, Julie works out that, if she has **$329 000** in superannuation when she retires, she can expect the following outcomes:

- a retirement income of around **$32 000** a year from the age of 60 until the age of 87 (27 years). From age 60 to age 67, Julie relies on super and private savings, then she is eligible for nearly a full Age Pension from age 67. From the age of 87, Julie will rely solely on the Age Pension

- alternatively, if Julie wants her money to last until she's 100, then she will have to accept a lower income of just over **$29 000** a year, with nearly a full Age Pension from age 67. What this means is that Julie can expect a regular income for 37 years, increasing by 3 per cent each year to allow for inflation.

Julie considers this an excellent outcome, considering she is planning to retire early, and will not have access to the Age Pension for the first seven years of her retirement.

Table 7.2: Julie's super balance if she does nothing, a little, a lot or heaps and retires at 60, or retires at 67 (age 35, $15000 starting account balance, income $50000 a year)

Julie (from age 35)	Doing nothing (9% SG only)		SG plus making own after-tax contributions	
Super contributions	Until age 60 $	Until age 67 $	Until age 60 $	Until age 67 $
Doing nothing				
SG only	198000	290000	n/a	n/a
Non-concessional (after-tax) contributions				
Doing a little				
SG + $1000 a year	n/a	n/a	245000	359000
Doing more				
SG + $2000 a year	n/a	n/a	287000	421000
Doing a lot				
SG + $3000 a year	n/a	n/a	329000	484000
Doing heaps				
SG + $5000 a year	n/a	n/a	412000	609000

Note: See the appendix for table assumptions.

Doing a lot and retiring at 67 means Julie has a $484000 nest egg

Julie is now motivated about her retirement planning and wonders what type of income she could enjoy if she worked until the age of 67 (her Age Pension age), and made her own contributions of **$3000** each year. Her final retirement balance works out to be **$484000** (see table 7.2).

Using the MoneySmart retirement planner calculator, Julie finds out that with **$484000** at retirement, she could enjoy an income of:

- **$45000** a year (including a part Age Pension) until the age of 87 — substantially more than the income needed for a comfortable lifestyle, as defined by the Retirement Standard (see the box on p. 103). In fact, $45000 a year works out to be nearly 110 per cent of her current after-tax income of **$41 250** (for the 2011–12 year; see the appendix for income tax rates for later years).

• **$41 250** a year in today's dollars (including a part Age Pension) until the age of 92, if Julie wants the same after-tax income that she enjoys today.

Julie's attitude to retirement planning has now completely changed. She realises that retirement won't be such a hardship after all, especially if she also increases her superannuation contributions closer to retirement. Julie can expect a comfortable retirement if she does a little planning.

Case study 3 (age 45): Sahn is sitting pretty for her retirement

Julie is stoked and tells another friend, Sahn, how easy it can be to plan for retirement. Sahn, aged 45, has only $35 000 in super and thinks the retirement stuff is all too hard. She expects to go on working until she dies, just to survive. Julie shows her the MoneySmart superannuation calculator and suggests that Sahn may want to work until at least the age of 67 (her Age Pension age), which means Sahn has another 22 years to accumulate retirement savings.

Doing nothing for 22 years delivers Sahn a $212 000 nest egg

Sahn, who also earns **$50 000** a year, finds out that her employer's annual $4500 super contributions can deliver her **$212 000** in today's dollars by the time she reaches 67 (see table 7.3). Incredible, she thinks, for doing nothing except turning up for work! Sahn appreciates that when she retires at 67 she would still be entitled to a substantial part Age Pension, and probably even a full Age Pension because she would be claiming the Age Pension with her partner, Alfredo: the Age Pension rate, and the Age Pension assets test threshold is higher for a couple (see chapter 11). Table 7.3 summarises Sahn's retirement options.

Although Sahn plans to be with her partner Alfredo when she retires, out of curiosity she works out what her retirement income would be if she was retiring as a single woman. Using the MoneySmart retirement planner calculator, Sahn estimates that if she relied on SG only, her **$212 000** final balance could give her an annual retirement income as a single person of around **$32 000** in today's dollars, until the age of 87 (including a substantial part Age Pension).

Doing a lot for 22 years delivers Sahn a $320 000 nest egg

Sahn wonders what her super balance would be if she contributed some of her own money to her super fund. She looks at two options — paying in $3000 or $5000.

- *$3000 a year in contributions.* If Sahn started contributing 6 per cent of her salary — $3000 — as non-concessional (after-tax) contributions, Sahn would also be entitled to a small co-contribution from the government, and at age 67 her super balance would be **$320 000** (see table 7.3). As a single person, her **$320 000** super balance can deliver Sahn a retirement income of around **$37 000** (including a part Age Pension) until the age of 87, or around **$32 000** a year if she wants her money to last until she turns 100.

- *$5000 a year in contributions (doing heaps).* If she boosts her annual non-concessional (after-tax) contributions to $5000 (10 per cent of her salary, or about $100 a week), for the next 22 years, then her final retirement balance could be around **$390 000** (see table 7.3) delivering her around **$40 000** a year (including a part Age Pension).

Table 7.3: Sahn's super balance and retirement income based on doing nothing, a lot, or heaps, retiring at 67 (single), or retiring at 67 (as a couple) (age 45, $15 000 starting account balance, earns $50 000 a year)

Sahn (from age 45)	Final retirement amount (at age 67) $	Annual tax-free retirement income $			
Super contributions		As a single person		As part of a couple	
		Until 87	Until 100	Until 87	Until 100
Doing nothing					
SG only	212 000	32 000	29 000	43 000	39 000
Non-concessional (after-tax) contributions					
Doing a little					
SG + $1000	251 000	34 000	30 000	45 000	41 000
Doing more					
SG + $2000	286 000	36 000	31 500	47 000	43 000
Doing a lot					
SG + $3000	320 000	37 000	32 000	48 000	44 000
Doing heaps					
SG + $5000	390 000	40 000	34 000	52 000	46 000

Note: See appendix for table assumptions.

Retiring as a couple can mean more Age Pension

Sahn is expecting to be with her partner when she retires so she's in for a pleasant surprise when calculating her retirement income. For simplicity, we'll assume that her partner is the same age, has no assets and no superannuation. If eligible, as a couple, they can apply for the Age Pension couple rate. Sahn looks at the following options:

- *Doing nothing — SG only.* According to the MoneySmart retirement planner, if Sahn makes no super contributions and relies solely on her employer's SG contributions plus earnings, then her retirement balance of **$212 000** (see table 7.3 on p. 107) can deliver Sahn and Alfredo a retirement income of around **$43 000** a year (including a full Age Pension), from the age of 67 until the age of 87. If Sahn wants her savings to last until she reaches 100, then she can reduce her annual income to around **$39 000** a year. Easy!

- *Doing a lot — making $3000 a year in non-concessional contributions.* If Sahn makes after-tax contributions of $3000 a year in addition to her employer's SG contributions, then her final retirement balance at age 67 is **$320 000** (see table 7.3). This amount can deliver Sahn and Alfredo an annual retirement income of around **$48 000** a year (including nearly a full Age Pension) — close to 100 per cent of Sahn's current before-tax salary, until age 87. If Sahn and her partner want their savings to last until they turn 100, then they will have to accept a lower annual income — around **$44 000** a year (including nearly a full Age Pension). Sahn is impressed: she will have a tax-free income in retirement that is larger than her current after-tax income of **$41 250** (for the 2011–12 year).

- *Doing heaps — making $5000 a year in non-concessional contributions.* If Sahn makes $5000 a year in after-tax contributions, then her final balance of **$390 000** (see table 7.3) can deliver Sahn and Alfredo an annual income of around **$52 000** a year (including nearly a full Age Pension), until the age of 87, close to the Retirement Standard's comfortable lifestyle (see p. 103), and more than 100 per cent of Sahn's current salary. Alternatively, they can choose to live on **$46 000** a year (including nearly a full Age Pension) until the age of 100.

Sahn is incredulous that she is going to be so financially comfortable when she retires. She runs the numbers through the MoneySmart superannuation and retirement planner calculators again, just to be sure.

Case study 4 (age 55): Lily's loving her new retirement plan

Sahn chats to her friend Lily about her new optimistic view on the marvels of her superannuation account. Lily, aged 55, is philosophical about her own financial position. She has spent most of her life rearing her children and, until now, worked in low-paid jobs casually and part time before getting divorced late in life. She has $70 000 in super, which she understands will mean that she can get the full Age Pension plus a few thousand extra each year from her superannuation savings. Lily is forgetting one thing. She hasn't retired yet, which means she still has 10 years of compulsory employer super contributions to be paid into her super account. Lily also now earns $50 000 a year, which means just for turning up for work her employer contributes $4500 to her super each year.

Doing nothing delivers Lily a retirement nest egg of $149 000

By doing nothing except turning up for work, Lily should have **$149 000** (see table 7.4, overleaf) when she retires at age 65 (her Age Pension age). She uses the MoneySmart retirement planner calculator and finds out that she can receive just over **$28 000** a year as income in retirement, including nearly a full Age Pension until the age of 87 — the average life expectancy for a 65-year-old female. After reaching 87 years of age, Lily can then expect to live on the full Age Pension only.

If Lily wants her money to last longer, she can drop her annual income to **$27 000** a year (including nearly a full Age Pension) and enjoy that level of income until the age of 95, or drop it again to **$26 000** (including nearly a full Age Pension) and enjoy that income until the grand old age of 100.

Doing a lot gives Lily $30 000 a year, from a $188 000 lump sum

Lily can improve her retirement lifestyle considerably by making her own super contributions. By using the MoneySmart superannuation and retirement planner calculators, Lily considers the following options:

- *Doing a lot — $3000 a year in after-tax contributions until age 65.* If Lily contributes $3000 a year of her own money as non-concessional (after-tax) contributions each year for the next 10 years, her super balance will be **$188 000** (see table 7.4) at the age of 65, giving her around $30 000 a year (including nearly a full Age Pension) in retirement, until age 87.

- *Doing heaps — $5000 a year in after-tax contributions until age 65.* If Lily contributes $5000 a year of her own money, her super balance will be $212 000 (see table 7.4), giving her around **$31 500** a year, until age 87, and **$28 500** a year until the age of 100, including nearly a full Age Pension.

Table 7.4: Lily's super balance and retirement income if she does nothing, a lot or heaps and retires at 65, or retires at 70 (age 55, $70 000 starting balance, income $50 000 a year)

Lily (from age 55)	Balance at age 65	Annual tax-free retirement income		Balance at age 70	Annual tax-free retirement income	
Super contribution	$	Until age 87 $	Until age 100 $	$	Until age 87 $	Until age 100 $
Doing nothing						
SG only	149 000	28 000	26 000	201 000	33 000	29 000
Non-concessional (after-tax) contributions						
Doing a little						
SG + $1000	164 000	29 000	27 000	225 000	34 000	30 000
Doing more						
SG + $2000	176 000	29 500	27 500	245 000	35 000	31 000
Doing a lot						
SG + $3000	188 000	30 000	28 000	265 000	36 500	31 500
Doing heaps						
SG + $5000	212 000	31 500	28 500	306 000	38 500	33 000

Note: See the appendix for table assumptions.

Working longer increases Lily's retirement income by $3000 a year

If Lily chose to work an extra five years — until age 70, then her employer's annual $4500 SG contribution plus her own contributions could mean the following:

- *Doing a lot — $3000 a year in after-tax contributions until age 70.* This option delivers a retirement balance of **$265 000**. Using the MoneySmart retirement planner calculator, Lily can expect a retirement income of around **$36 500** (including a substantial part Age Pension) in today's dollars, from the age of 70 until the age of 87. If she wants her savings to last until she is 100, then Lily can expect an annual income in retirement of around **$31 500** a year (including a substantial part Age Pension).

- *Doing heaps — $5000 a year in after-tax super contributions for 15 years.* In this case her super balance could be **$306 000**, giving her a retirement income of around **$38 500** (including a substantial part Age Pension), until age 87, or an income of **$33 000** (including a substantial part Age Pension) until the age of 100.

Good news alert no. 7: work breaks and super

It's not always possible to regularly contribute to a super fund, or to work continuously for 10, 20 or 30 years. What often happens, particularly for women, is that saving for retirement is a project left until after the kids have grown up, or when a marriage breaks up, or when the home loan is finally repaid. The superannuation rules are reasonably flexible to permit larger one-off after-tax super contributions in particular years. I explain the rules applying to superannuation contributions in chapters 6 and 10.

Chapter 8

Doing a lot: making $1 million is possible, but it takes a super plan

> 66 *Please Sir, I want some more.* 99

Oliver Twist *by Charles Dickens*

In chapter 4, I write about the ASFA study (which I refer to as the Retirement Standard) that researched the lives of actual retirees and determined that retirees can live a comfortable life on an income of around **$39 000** a year (for singles) or **$54 000** (for couples) after tax.

On this level of income, you can eat out regularly each week, use the internet and a mobile phone frequently, enjoy an occasional glass of wine (or possibly two quality bottles of wine a week, for couples), afford the top rate of private health cover, afford more expensive clothing and underwear, replace whitegoods when necessary, run an air-conditioner, buy magazines, enjoy regular Australian holidays and an overseas holiday once every five years.

Living on this level of income can deliver a worry-free and lovely lifestyle in retirement, but it is certainly not an extravagant lifestyle. For example, if you intend to travel overseas every year (rather than every five years when living a comfortable life), and enjoy a quality bottle of wine two or three times a week (rather than one quality bottle of wine, or two reasonable bottles, over a week), and maintain a luxury car or run a holiday home, then you may have to plan on living on more than **$39 000** (single) or **$54 000** (couple) a year.

The main reason I decided to write this book is to help women discover how they can accumulate wealth for retirement in a relatively pain-free way — by doing nothing other than turning up to work every day, by doing a little or by doing a lot. If you earn a higher income, then the strategies described in other chapters and in this chapter can be applied to build a $1 million retirement balance with minimal worry. If you earn a lower income and you want to reach for the stars, then it is still possible to realise your retirement dream, but you will need to actively plan to build your super savings now, or later in life, and potentially accumulate investments outside the super system as well.

> ## Tip
>
> When you retire, you're unlikely to have mortgage repayments (around 80 per cent of Australians own their own home in retirement), and you're unlikely to be making super contributions, so you have a strong chance of achieving a more expensive lifestyle than the one you're living on now by aiming for your current after-tax salary in retirement. If you do plan to enter retirement with a mortgage or other debts, or if you plan to rent a home in retirement, then you need to factor those extra costs into your retirement plans.

> ## Tip
>
> If you currently earn **$70 000** or less, you won't need anywhere near $1 million in retirement to maintain your current lifestyle. With the helping hand of the Age Pension and tax-free super benefits, you may be surprised by the amount of income needed to deliver you a worry-free financial future. For example, if you're part of a couple, you can achieve **$80 000** a year (including a part Age Pension) as tax-free retirement income (until age 87) if you have just over **$600 000** in super savings. I explain what tax-free income means for your retirement planning in this chapter.

Your retirement dream is closer than you think

Did you know that a tax-free income of **$54 000** in retirement is the equivalent to a before-tax salary of **$68 000** a year while you're working? After you remove the income tax of around $14 000 on a $68 000 salary, you're left with an after-tax income of **$54 040** (for the 2011–12 year), or **$54 353** (from 2012–13, subject to the legislation being passed). In other words, if you're earning $68 000 a year, you're really living on **$54 040** (for the 2011–12 year), once you deduct the annual income tax that you pay (see the appendix for income tax rates).

In retirement, you don't pay tax on your retirement income when your income is sourced from your savings within the super system, which means that if you want the same income in retirement that you enjoy today, then you should aim to match your current after-tax salary.

If you live within your means on your current salary, then your current after-tax income amount is a healthy retirement target, considering you will also not be making super contributions in retirement, and hopefully not making mortgage repayments.

Tip

If your retirement income is sourced entirely from your super savings then you can expect a tax-free retirement from the age of 60 (with the exception of some public servants). If your income in retirement is sourced partly from non-super income, or even, in some cases, sourced entirely from non-super income (subject to an upper income limit), then you can still look forward to a tax-free life when you retire after reaching your Age Pension age. The special tax concessions available on non-super income (including Age Pension payments) for Australians who have reached Age Pension age, especially when combined with tax-free super benefits, can help make your retirement worry-free and tax-free. (See chapter 11 for the tax rules in retirement, including the tax treatment of some benefits paid to public servants.)

In table 8.1 (overleaf), I outline a sample of working incomes and translate them into what those incomes mean when you remove the income tax payable. The after-tax income is a useful comparison when deciding on your retirement target income. You may want to read this section and table 8.1 a second time, because the concepts are a bit tricky, but fascinating.

For example, if you earn a salary of **$70 000**, then your after-tax salary works out to be **$55 450** (for 2011–12, or **$55 703** for 2012–13, subject to the legislation being passed). Using $55 450 as your target retirement income, you need **$710 000** as a single person to finance a tax-free retirement income of **$55 450** (including a part Age Pension) until the age of 87, according to the

MoneySmart retirement planner calculator. If you want this level of income until the age of 100, however, then you should aim for a retirement balance close to **$1 million**.

As a couple, you can enjoy a tax-free income of **$55 450** a year until the age of 100 with a retirement lump sum of **$660 000** (including a part Age Pension). If a couple has **$710 000** in savings, they can potentially enjoy a tax-free income in retirement of just over **$67 000** a year (including a part Age Pension), until age 87, which is equivalent to the couple living on around **$88 000** a year during their working life.

Tip

Lump sum amounts, annual retirement incomes and annual salaries quoted throughout this chapter are in today's dollars. Due to the effects of rising prices (inflation) over time, amounts quoted need to be adjusted back to what your money can buy today. I explain today's dollars in chapter 3.

Table 8.1: working out your retirement target—what is your current income worth as after-tax income?

Current salary $	Less income tax payable (for 2011–12) $	Equals after-tax salary/ retirement income target $	Total lump sum necessary to finance retirement income target until age 87 (includes Age Pension) $	
			Single person	Couple (combined lump sum)
30 000	3 600	27 400	205 000	Nil
40 000	5 550	34 450	265 000	90 000
50 000	8 750	41 250	410 000	245 000
60 000	11 450	48 550	610 000	385 000
70 000	14 550	55 450	710 000	525 000
80 000	17 550	62 450	845 000	610 000
90 000	21 250	68 750	955 000	745 000
100 000	24 950	75 050	1 million+*	885 000
120 000	32 350	87 650	1 million+*	1 million+*

Note: Due to tax changes planned to take effect from July 2012 (subject to the legislation being passed), the income tax bill at most income levels will be slightly lower from 2012–13, which means after-tax incomes will be slightly higher in future years. The lump sum amounts listed remain indicative for future years. See appendix for table assumptions.

*At this level of income, you can expect to receive some Age Pension in the later years of retirement, although table 8.2 is a more useful reference at these higher income levels.

Wanting more than $39 000 (single) or $54 000 (couple) a year in retirement, with no Age Pension

The Six-Step Wealth Check (see chapter 4) becomes even more relevant for those wanting a more luxurious lifestyle in retirement, or a lifestyle that is not supplemented by the Age Pension. As a quick refresher, the Six-Step Wealth Check involves:

- Step 1: Choose your lifestyle.

- Step 2: Calculate the cost of your chosen lifestyle, that is, your target retirement income.

- Step 3: Calculate the lump sum amount needed for your chosen lifestyle in retirement.

- Step 4: Do a financial stocktake today.

- Step 5: Do a financial stocktake for tomorrow.

- Step 6: Close the gap.

If you're already thinking that you want more than a comfortable lifestyle (more than **$39 000** a year for a single person and more than **$54 000** for a couple, according to the Retirement Standard), then I assume you have worked out the lifestyle that you want (step 1), and how much such a lifestyle is going to cost (step 2).

How much money will you need then, as a lump sum, to finance your chosen lifestyle in retirement (step 3)?

Table 8.2 (see p. 119) gives examples of a few aspirational retirement incomes and suggests target final account balances that you're likely to need to finance such an income until you reach the age of 87 (roughly, a female's average life expectancy at age 65 or 67), or until you reach the age of 100. Note that the earlier you retire the more money you will need to save for your given lifestyle in retirement.

No Age Pension

The lump sum amounts in table 8.2 assume that you will receive no Age Pension. I have included this table for those readers who want flexibility when choosing their retirement age, or flexibility about the other assets they may want to own, such as a holiday house, or other substantial assets in addition to a superannuation account. A holiday house, plus substantial super savings, may preclude you from claiming the Age Pension, because of the Age Pension assets test (see chapter 11).

If you're seeking a lifestyle that is significantly more than **$39 000** (single) or **$54 000** (couple) a year free of tax, then table 8.2 demonstrates that your target retirement amount is heading towards **$1 million** and beyond, particularly if you want to retire before you reach 65 or 67, and if you may not be eligible to access a part Age Pension as a supplement to your super income.

For example, consider the following **$1 million** scenarios outlined in table 8.2:

- If you want to live on **$80 000** a year and retire at age 60, then you will need a **$1.36 million** lump sum on retirement for your money to last until the age of 87 (after the age of 87, you would rely solely on the Age Pension). If you want **$80 000** a year until you reach the age of 100, that is, for 40 years, then you will need a retirement balance of **$1.64 million**. The Age Pension is generally available at nearly all income levels listed in table 8.2 once an individual reaches the later years of retirement, although table 8.2 does not include Age Pension entitlements.

- If you want to live on **$80 000** a year and you're willing to wait until the age of 65 to retire, then the lump sum you will need is **$1.25 million** for the money to last until the age of 87, or **$1.56 million** if you want your savings to last until the age of 100.

Tip

A tax-free income of **$80 000** a year (retirement income is sourced from superannuation savings) is the equivalent to earning about **$110 000** a year if you had to pay income tax on your income (see appendix for an outline of income tax rates).

Age Pension is likely for most, at some stage

At the lower income levels set out in table 8.2, singles may be entitled to a part Age Pension, which means the lump sums needed on retirement could be considerably lower than are listed in table 8.2 (see table 8.1 on p. 116). For example, if you're saving as a single person, then you're likely to secure a retirement income of **$50 000** a year, including a part Age Pension, with a lump sum amount of around **$640 000** (until the age of 87), assuming you have reached the Age Pension age of 67 (see chapter 11).

In the later years of retirement, as you use up your super savings, as a single person you're likely to be able to claim a part Age Pension at some of the higher income levels, which may mean that the lump sum required on retirement will be lower than the amounts outlined in table 8.2.

If you're saving as a couple, then you're likely to be able to claim a part Age Pension at the $50 000, $60 000, $70 000, $80 000, $90 000 and $100 000 annual income levels represented in table 8.2, assuming you have reached your Age Pension age. For example, a couple may need only **$400 000** (retiring at age 67) to **$410 000** (retiring at age 65) to enjoy an annual retirement income of **$51 000** a year (until age 87), because they would be eligible for a couple's part Age Pension. Same-sex couples are also eligible for the couple Age Pension rate.

Table 8.2: how much money is enough for a worry-free retirement, with no Age Pension?

Annual retirement income (paid as tax-free super benefits)	If retire at age 60, and money lasts until:		If retire at age 65, and money lasts until:		If retire at age 67, and money lasts until:	
	Age 87 $	Age 100 $	Age 87 $	Age 100 $	Age 87 $	Age 100 $
50 000	850 000	1.03 m	760 000	970 000	720 000	950 000
60 000	1.02 m	1.23 m	910 000	1.17 m	860 000	1.14 m
70 000	1.19 m	1.44 m	1.06 m	1.36 m	1.00 m	1.33 m
80 000	1.36 m	1.64 m	1.25 m	1.56 m	1.15 m	1.55 m
100 000	1.70 m	2.05 m	1.55 m	1.95 m	1.45 m	1.90 m
150 000	2.55 m	3.10 m	2.27 m	2.92 m	2.15 m	2.85 m
200 000	3.40 m	4.10 m	3.03 m	3.88 m	2.90 m	3.80 m

Note: The amounts in table 8.2 were calculated using the MoneySmart account-based pension calculator. The 'm' stands for million. See appendix for table assumptions.

Tip

Chapter 9 shows how you can combine some of the aspirational retirement incomes listed in table 8.2 with the Age Pension to help you reach for the stars with less money.

Winning lotto is not the only way to score $1 million

When most Australians talk about receiving $1 million they are usually referring to winning lotto and what they would do with such a financial windfall. The magical million dollars seems to evoke dreams and possibilities for the future. Most Australians need a lot less than $1 million to change their financial future and, as I have already shown, you don't need $1 million in today's dollars to have a nice life in retirement.

The question that usually comes to mind at this stage is: how do I get from thinking about my $1 million retirement dream to making it happen?

> ## Tip
>
> There is a delightful secret to wealth accumulation that many successful investors discover: once you have a plan in place, you don't have to do most of the work—your investments do the work for you.

In terms of superannuation, the trustees of your superannuation fund invest your super money on your behalf, and your super fund's investments earn interest (if cash or term deposit investments) or dividends (if share investments) or distributions (if real estate investment trusts or other types of investment vehicles).

After a small amount of tax is paid on those earnings by your super fund, the fund then reinvests these earnings by buying more investments (also known as assets), and then these additional investments also deliver income to your super fund, and hopefully the assets increase in value over time.

If your super fund sells any assets (investments), your fund receives capital gains when it sells the asset for more than it paid for it. Sometimes it may suffer a capital loss, when it sells a fund asset for less than it paid for the asset.

Of course, having investments work for you does not mean that you can forget about your wealth plans, especially if you have expectations of a luxurious life in retirement. You have many opportunities to help your wealth plans along, especially your superannuation plans.

You can change your financial future — dramatically — by changing any one of the nine elements discussed in this chapter.

Change your financial future, in at least nine ways

You have a lot of control over what your financial future is going to look like. You don't have to use the superannuation system to accumulate wealth, or use only the super system to build wealth, but superannuation is definitely one of the easiest ways to save for retirement.

Doing a little in terms of superannuation can improve your lifestyle in retirement and give you a worry-free financial future. Doing a lot can radically transform what your life in retirement is going to look like.

Continue reading this chapter to discover ways to close the gap between your lifestyle expectations in retirement, and what your current plans (if any) are going to deliver. (Chapter 9 includes the stories of four women who expect to add hundreds of thousands of dollars to their final superannuation balance by making a simple and achievable super plan, and by changing one or more of the following variables.)

Tip

The rest of this chapter will help you even more when you have gone through step 4 (financial stocktake of your super savings, as of today) and step 5 (what your super savings will be tomorrow if you continue doing what you're currently doing) of my Six-Step Wealth Check, and discovered that you have a gap between what you want in retirement, and what your existing savings and strategies (if any) will deliver you on retirement. (If you want some help working through steps 4 and 5, then check out the case studies in chapters 5, 7 and 9.)

Before committing to any major superannuation strategy, it is important to understand the key drivers that grow your super account over time, including the following nine elements:

1 *Your level of income during your working life.* Your level of income can affect your wealth accumulation plans in at least three ways. Your employer contributes the equivalent of 9 per cent of your salary to your super fund under the SG rules, which means the higher your income, the larger your employer's contribution will be, subject to an upper salary limit. Second, if you're self-employed, then you must take positive action to build your

super benefit. Third, if you enjoy an above-average income, you may have higher expectations for your lifestyle in retirement than a woman on a lower income, and you're likely to have more disposable income to redirect to superannuation or other types of savings plans.

2   *Your tax bill.* The more tax you have to pay on your personal income, and other investments, the less money is available to invest for your financial future. Tax-friendly investments such as superannuation can help Australians reach their financial goals faster because, depending on your income, less money is snaffled by the taxman. The higher your income, the more likely that you will choose to make before-tax (concessional) super contributions, rather than after-tax (non-concessional) contributions, because you can save thousands of dollars in tax this way (see chapter 10). Remember, most retirees can expect to pay no tax in retirement if their savings are in the super system.

3   *Amount of superannuation contributions — one-off or regular contributions.* If you add more money to an existing pool of money, you will obviously have a bigger pool of money. Likewise, if you make additional super contributions, you can expect your superannuation balance to grow faster. You also have another element boosting your super savings — compound earnings. Your superannuation account receives returns or earnings from your super fund's investments, and then those earnings are reinvested with the balance of your super account, giving you even more returns. Compound earnings, plus regular additional contributions, or even one-off contributions, can supercharge the growth of your super account over time. (See chapter 10 for more information.)

4   *Years of contributions.* The longer the time frame in which you make regular contributions, the more money is invested over time for your retirement. More contributions from you (and your employer) means a larger pool of savings, and your super account reaps the benefits of compound earnings for a longer period of time, creating a larger final super balance.

5   *Rate of investment return.* The return, or earnings, on your superannuation account or other non-super savings is the key contributor to wealth accumulation. If you want higher returns, you generally have to take higher risks, which can mean investment losses in some years. For some

individuals, losing money is too stressful and they would rather opt for an asset allocation that delivers a moderate long-term return, and invest for a longer period, or contribute more regularly, or even delay retirement to accumulate a larger super balance. In nearly all case studies throughout this book, I use 7 per cent after fees and taxes as the assumed rate of return (see chapter 10 for more information on how you could adjust your super account's long-term investment return).

6   *Years that you hold investments or hold your super account.* Time is the key when accumulating wealth the easy way. You let compound earnings weave their magic and, if you choose, you can rev up your superannuation savings with additional super contributions. If you don't have time on your side, however, then you may have no choice but to contribute more money, or take more risks when investing, or decide to accept a less costly lifestyle in retirement. Note that taking more risks also means that you have a higher chance of losing some of your savings.

7   *Fees.* Fees, like taxes, are the hidden enemies of investors, although fees are necessary if you're planning to rely on someone else to invest your super money. Even when you choose to run your own super fund (known as a self managed super fund) you will still encounter fees. The trick is to manage the amount of fees that you have to pay. The key to accumulating wealth, however, is the return on your investments — maximising the long-term return *after* fees and taxes (see chapter 3).

8   *Retirement age.* If you retire too early, you can miss out on important extra years for accumulating wealth for your retirement. A further disadvantage when you retire too early, is that you need to save more for your retirement because you will need to finance more years in retirement. Generally speaking, the earlier you retire, the smaller your super payout is, and the longer it has to last. In comparison, the later you retire, the larger your super account balance and you then also have fewer years in retirement to finance with your lump sum.

9   *Working (and contributing to super) in retirement.* If you're willing to continue working when you retire, especially if you plan to retire before Age Pension age, the amount of money that you need on retirement is a lot less, because you're providing a second income stream sourced from your work income. If this is an option you're considering, then you need to be very particular about your plans, because most individuals

choosing this option work only for the first few years of their retirement, and then rely solely on superannuation and non-super savings, and the Age Pension (if they are eligible).

Tip

You may also receive an inheritance later in life, or other lump sum (such as the proceeds from a divorce settlement) that you can put towards your wealth accumulation plans. If you're married or in a de facto relationship, don't forget to factor in your partner's superannuation benefits. Even if the relationship breaks up, you're entitled to up to half of your partner's superannuation benefits, and likewise he or she is entitled to a share of your super benefits. I explain what happens to superannuation benefits when a relationship breaks down on my free website, SuperGuide at <www.superguide.com.au>.

Chapter 9

Case studies—four women create $1 million nest eggs

" *There are people who have money and people who are rich.* "

Coco Chanel, French fashion designer

In this chapter, you can read about four women who have worked out what they want for their lives in retirement, and then created a million-dollar plan to make it happen.

Before you read on, I do want to make an important point. Although the idea of a million-dollar retirement may sound enticing, most Australians don't need $1 million in retirement to maintain the lifestyle they enjoyed during their working life. Even when you expect to have similar costs in retirement as you incur while you're working, the fact that you will pay no income tax in retirement if you keep your savings in the superannuation system can immediately improve your financial circumstances for retirement.

If you earn up to **$68 000** a year while you're working, then you're likely to discover that a comfortable lifestyle on **$54 000** a year in retirement (see chapters 4 and 8) offers an equivalent or better lifestyle than the one you enjoy now, once you remove the tax that you pay (see appendix for income tax rates). If you earn less than **$68 000** and you're able to finance a **$54 000** a year income in retirement, then you can expect a much higher standard of living than your current lifestyle.

Tip

The retirement incomes quoted in this chapter are tax-free incomes, sourced from retirement savings held in the superannuation system. If your retirement income is sourced entirely from your super savings then you can expect a tax-free retirement from the age of 60 (with the exception of some public servants). If your income in retirement is sourced partly from non-super income, then you can still plan for a tax-free life, although you will need to have reached your Age Pension age, and manage your financial affairs closely. The special tax concessions available on non-super income (including Age Pension payments) for Australians who have reached Age Pension age, especially when combined with tax-free super benefits, can deliver a tax-free retirement. (See chapter 11 for the tax rules in retirement.)

Now, let me introduce you to the four women, ranging in age from 30 to 55, and their aspirations for retirement:

- Kim, age 30, earns $80 000 a year (case study 1 on p. 128). She wants to live on the same income ($80 000) when she retires. Her partner, Sam, is an artist and part-time teacher. Kim's current super account balance is $40 000. (See page 128.)

- Sal, age 35, earns $70 000 a year (case study 2 on p. 133). Her husband, Vladimir, earns $80 000 a year. Sal and Vladimir want to live on $100 000 a year, when they retire. If she is on her own, Sal wants to live on $60 000 a year. Her current super account balance is $20 000. (See page 133.)

- Maree, age 45, is recently divorced (case study 3 on p. 139). She wants to live on $60 000 a year in retirement. Maree currently has $110 000 in super (sourced predominantly from an inheritance). She has started a new job earning $120 000 a year plus super. (See page 139.)

- Julianne, age 55, is self-employed and a widow (case study 4 on p. 144). She wants to live on $60 000 a year in retirement. She has $500 000 in super, and now earns $90 000 a year plus super. In short, she has to double her money in 10 years. Julianne discovers this outcome is possible. (See page 144.)

> **Tip**
>
> In this chapter, I used the MoneySmart account-based pension calculator, superannuation calculator and retirement planner calculator to compile the lump sum figures and retirement incomes in the text and tables. The assumptions used appear in the appendix where I also explain the calculators, and how they can help you plan for a worry-free financial future.

The four women featured in the case studies in this chapter make concessional (before-tax) contributions to boost their super savings, using a salary sacrifice arrangement. The strategy of salary sacrifice works in the following way. You ask your employer whether you can redirect some of your before-tax salary into super contributions, and then you pay income tax only on the balance of your salary. You end up paying less income tax, while you boost your super contributions. Your super contributions are then subject to 15 per cent contributions tax, which means salary sacrificing can be tax-effective when you pay more than 15 per cent tax on non-super income — earn more than $37 000 a year (for the 2011–12 financial year, or from 2012–13, earn more than $18 000, or $20 542 when you take into account the low income tax offset, subject to the legislation being passed). If you're self-employed, you can make tax-deductible super contributions and enjoy the same tax benefits as the four women in the case studies using salary sacrificing. I explain salary sacrifice and tax-deductible contributions in chapter 10 (see tip 11 on p. 165–8).

> **Tip**
>
> Lump sum amounts, annual retirement incomes and annual salaries quoted throughout this chapter are in today's dollars. I explained today's dollars in chapter 3.

Case study 1 (age 30): Kim's high expectations can be met

Kim is 30 years of age and already earns $80 000 plus super a year. She expects to be on this income or higher for most of her working life. Her partner, Sam, an artist and part-time teacher, will be the spouse taking a break from work when Kim has children. She likes the life she has when earning $80 000 a year and wants a similar life when she retires. Kim's current super account balance is $40 000. Any superannuation that her partner Sam has will be used to clear the mortgage (if any), or spent on the house, when they retire.

Sam's teaching income is currently used for mortgage repayments and Kim's $80 000 income is used for everyday costs and lifestyle expenses, and for holidays. Although Kim will take on the mortgage repayments when Sam looks after the prospective children full time, Kim has big plans for the couple's retirement and believes that she will be able to make voluntary super contributions in addition to her employer's super contributions. Kim believes that they will need $80 000 a year for retirement and she is willing to work until the age of 67 to make it happen. They would prefer to retire at age 60, or even 65, but Kim realises that, to enjoy such a high income in retirement, she may need to delay her retirement.

Kim is aware that she won't have any mortgage payments or superannuation contributions in retirement, or any tax bills if she keeps her money in the super system when she retires. That means she won't need **$80 000** in retirement to enjoy the same lifestyle that she is enjoying now — a tax-free income of **$62 450** (for the 2011–12 year, or **$62 453** from 2012–13, subject to the legislation being passed) is the equivalent of $80 000 in salary before income tax is deducted.

If Kim and Sam truly want an income of **$80 000** in retirement from age 67, then they will need to plan for a likely retirement savings target ranging from **$1.15 million** to **$1.55 million** (assuming no Age Pension entitlements) depending on how long they want their money to last (see table 9.1).

Table 9.1: how much money is enough? Kim is aged 30, receives no Age Pension and wants a retirement income of $80 000 a year

Kim's target retirement income $	Retiring at 60, and money lasts until:		Retiring at 65, and money lasts until:		Retiring at 67, and money lasts until:	
	Age 87 $	Age 100 $	Age 87 $	Age 100 $	Age 87 $	Age 100 $
80 000	1.36 m	1.64 m	1.25 m	1.56 m	1.15 m	1.55 m

Note: The lump sum amounts assume no Age Pension entitlements. For other table assumptions see the appendix.

If the couple want to retire at age 60, on **$80 000** a year, then the savings target will range from **$1.36 million** (lasting until age 87) to **$1.64 million** (lasting until age 100), assuming no Age Pension entitlements.

Doing nothing (SG only) gives Kim $64 000 a year in retirement

Kim is off to a very good start with her retirement planning simply by keeping her job. Her employer must contribute **$7200** each year (9 per cent SG) to Kim's super account, which means that by the time she reaches the age of 67, Kim's **$40 000** starting superannuation account balance will have grown to **$660 000**—just for turning up for work.

Assuming no Age Pension (although at this level of assets a couple can expect to receive a generous part Age Pension), Kim and Sam can expect a retirement income of **$46 000** a year until the age of 87, or **$35 000** a year until the age of 100 (see table 9.2 on p. 131).

If Kim and Sam claim the Age Pension on retirement, then the **$660 000** can go a lot further. The couple could expect a retirement income of **$64 000** a year until the age of 87 (including a part Age Pension), or **$54 000** a year until the age of 100 (including a part Age Pension—see table 9.2). Not bad! For a couple, a part Age Pension is possible even when a couple have close to **$1 million** in assets (see chapter 11 for more information on the Age Pension entitlements).

What Kim didn't realise is that the **$64 000** a year in retirement that she can expect for doing nothing is a higher after-tax income than she lives on today—**$80 000** a year less income tax payable equals **$62 450** (for the 2011–12 year, or **$62 453** from 2012–13, subject to the legislation being passed). Kim is bemused by this discovery and wonders whether they really need $80 000 a year in retirement. Even so, doing nothing but turning up for work is not Kim's preferred option at the moment, because she doesn't want to include Age Pension entitlements in her planning.

Doing a little delivers Kim $1 million, and $80 000 a year

Kim has plenty of options in terms of superannuation strategies but she likes simplicity. She chooses to make concessional (before-tax) contributions every year of her working life, by entering a salary sacrifice arrangement with her employer. Kim looks at her spending and believes that she can easily redirect some of her salary to her superannuation account. Kim decides to redirect $5000 of her salary, and saves $1500 in income tax, because that would have been the tax payable on $5000 of Kim's salary for the 2011–12 year. Kim's super fund still has to deduct 15 per cent tax ($750) from Kim's super contribution, but that beats 30 per cent tax on non-super income (or 32.5 per cent tax on non-super income from 2012–13 year, subject to the legislation being passed). In short, by salary sacrificing, Kim's after-tax income has been reduced by only $3500 (for 2011–12), but her super account is boosted by $4250.

If Kim continues this strategy for her working life she can expect to have **$1 006 000** in her super account at age 67. This amount at retirement can deliver Kim and Sam around **$70 000** a year in retirement until the age of 87, or around **$53 000** a year until the age of 100, assuming no Age Pension is paid throughout retirement. Not bad for a simple strategy, implemented early. Receiving a **$70 000** annual tax-free income in retirement is the equivalent of earning around **$93 000** a year while working, due to the impact of income tax (see appendix for income tax rates).

At the time of writing, with more than **$1 million** in assets, Kim and Sam would be ineligible for the Age Pension on retirement. The couple are surprised, however, that as they spend their super savings during retirement, they will become eligible for a part Age Pension — sooner than they think! If the couple claim the Age Pension when eligible, by doing a little Kim and Sam can expect **$80 500** a year until the age of 87 (including a part Age Pension from the age of 68 rather than 67), or **$64 500** a year until the age of 100 (including a part Age Pension from the age of 68 — see table 9.2).

Kim thinks this is an amazing result for such little effort — she has already reached her retirement target with only a little change from what she is doing today! Even so, Kim wants to enjoy **$80 000** a year until the age of 100, although she doesn't expect to live to the age of 100. She also worries that the government may change the Age Pension rules for a couple with **$1 million** or more in assets, and doesn't want to include Age Pension entitlements in her planning. She considers increasing the amount she salary sacrifices.

Doing heaps delivers Kim her retirement dream of $80 000 a year, until age 100

If Kim chooses to do a lot towards her retirement savings she could increase her concessional contributions through salary sacrifice to **$7500** a year (in addition to her employer's contributions of **$7200**). She can then expect a final retirement balance at age 67 of **$1 179 000**, which can deliver Kim and Sam an annual retirement income of **$82 000** until the age of 87 (assuming no Age Pension entitlements)—exceeding her retirement income target of **$80 000** a year. If Kim wants this level of income to last until she reaches the age of 100, however, then she may have to make larger contributions. A retirement balance of **$1 179 000** delivers only **$62 000** a year (no Age Pension entitlements) in retirement until the age of 100 (see table 9.2).

Table 9.2: Kim's super balance and retirement income if she does nothing, a little, a lot or heaps (age 30, $40 000 starting account balance, income $80 000 a year)

| Kim (age 30) | | Annual tax-free retirement income | | | | |
| | | Until age 87 | | Until age 100 | | |
Super contributions	Retirement balance at age 67	No Age Pension $	Part Age Pension $	No Age Pension $	Part Age Pension $
Doing nothing					
SG only	660 000	46 000	**64 000**	35 000	**54 000**
Concessional (before-tax) contributions					
Doing a little					
SG +$5000 a year (salary sacrifice)	1 006 000	70 000	**80 500**	53 000	**64 500**
Doing a lot					
SG + $7500 a year (salary sacrifice	1 179 000	82 000	**See adviser**	62 000	**See adviser**
Doing heaps					
SG + $10 000 a year (salary sacrifice)	1 352 000	94 000	**See adviser**	71 000	**See adviser**

Note: The MoneySmart retirement planning calculator doesn't cater for retirement lump sums beyond $1 million. If you expect to receive a lump sum of this size, and you're hoping to claim a part Age Pension at a later stage in your retirement, then it's worth chatting to a financial adviser about your retirement options. For table assumptions see the appendix.

Kim will have to do heaps if she wants to live on **$80 000** a year in retirement until the age of 100. She could consider increasing her salary sacrifice contributions. For example:

- If she increased her contributions to **$10 000** a year (roughly $195 each week), her final retirement balance could be **$1 352 000**, giving her **$94 000** a year (assuming no Age Pension) until the age of 87, or **$71 000** a year until the age of 100, or **$80 000** a year (assuming no Age Pension) until the age of 93.

- For Kim to accumulate enough savings (**$1 550 000**) to deliver her **$80 000** a year until the age of 100 (assuming no Age Pension entitlements), she could make **$13 000** a year (about $250 a week) in salary sacrifice contributions, or choose to substantially boost her super contributions at a later date.

Kim has plenty of super options

Kim is not yet willing to commit an additional $10 000 a year (and definitely not $13 000) to her super account — she thinks contributing $7500 at the moment is a reasonable compromise between enjoying their lifestyle today but also saving for their future lifestyle. But Kim is confident that, as she gets closer to retirement, and she secures more senior roles at work, then making a few extra contributions from year to year will mean they will reach the target amount without much change to their current lifestyle. Kim is relieved that she took the time to do her Six-Step Wealth Check.

Kim now knows that her retirement savings strategy of doing a lot — making **$7500** each year (about $145 each week) in voluntary before-tax super contributions will deliver a higher income than she receives now — **$82,000** a year — until the age of 87 (assuming no Age Pension). Alternatively, if Kim and Sam claim the Age Pension, they can expect to enjoy **$80 000** a year free of tax in retirement (until the age of 87) by doing a little (SG + **$5000** salary sacrifice).

Kim is also aware that if she does nothing (relying only on her employer's compulsory contributions to super), she can still secure a similar after-tax income to the after-tax income she enjoys today. By simply turning up for work for the next 37 years, Kim will have enough super savings to deliver a tax-free income in retirement of at least **$62 450** (including part Age Pension) until age 87, which is the same as her working income of **$80 000**, after income tax (for 2011–12) is deducted from her salary.

Case study 2 (age 35): Sal splits her super strategy with her spouse

Sal is 35 and wants to live on $100 000 a year in retirement with her husband, Vladimir. She has just started a new job and is earning $70 000 a year, after a seven-year break to raise their children. Vladimir, also aged 35, earns $80 000 a year. Sal believes that, together with her husband, they can make this retirement income a reality by the time they retire at age 67. She also wants to work out whether she can accumulate enough savings on her own for a retirement income of $60 000 a year, just in case she and Vladimir don't remain together—Sal's parents divorced in their fifties, and she wants to be practical about something as important as her life in retirement.

Vladimir has $40 000 in his super account, while Sal has $20 000 in her super account, and they both plan to retire at age 67.

If Sal and Vladimir want an income of **$100 000** in retirement from age 67, then they'll need to plan for a likely retirement savings target range of **$1.45 million** to **$1.9 million** (assuming no Age Pension entitlements), depending on how long they want their money to last (see table 9.3). If the couple want to retire at age 60, on **$100 000** a year, then the savings target will range between **$1.7 million** (lasting until age 87) and **$2.05 million** (lasting until age 100). I also provide target lump sums at retirement to deliver **$60 000** a year in retirement (if Sal lives on her own in retirement) in table 9.3.

Table 9.3 assumes they will not receive any Age Pension, but Sal and Vladimir can potentially expect a small part Age Pension in the later years of their retirement, as part of their **$100 000** a year retirement income. Sal can expect a part Age Pension in retirement if she is living on her own and is aiming for a retirement income of **$60 000** a year.

Table 9.3 how much money is enough? Sal is aged 35 and wants $100 000 a year (if part of couple), or $60 000 a year (if single), with no Age Pension

Sal's target retirement income $	Retiring at 60, and money lasts until:		Retiring at 65, and money lasts until:		Retiring at 67, and money lasts until:	
	Age 87 $	Age 100 $	Age 87 $	Age 100 $	Age 87 $	Age 100 $
100 000	1.70 m	2.05 m	1.55 m	1.95 m	1.45 m	1.90 m
60 000	1.02 m	1.23 m	910 000	1.17 m	860 000	1.14 m

Note: The lump sum amounts assume no Age Pension entitlements. For other table assumptions see the appendix.

Doing nothing (SG only) gives Sal and Vladimir $76000 a year in retirement

If Sal and Vladimir do nothing but rely on compulsory employer contributions (SG) they can expect the following outcomes:

- If Sal relies only on her employer's compulsory contributions, by the time she reaches age 67 her account balance will be **$403000**.

- If Vladimir makes no contributions of his own, and relies only on his employer's compulsory contributions, then he can expect to have **$518000** at age 67.

- The couple will then have a total of **$921000** between them just for turning up for work.

Assuming no Age Pension (although with this level of assets a couple can expect to receive a small part Age Pension), by starting one or more superannuation pensions (income streams) with **$921000** at age 67, Sal and Vladimir can expect **$64000** a year until the age of 87, or **$48000** a year until the age of 100 (see table 9.4).

If Sal and Vladimir claim the Age Pension on retirement, then their **$921000** in super can deliver a higher annual retirement income, even though their super balance is near the Age Pension assets threshold for a couple, when eligibility for an Age Pension stops. The couple can expect **$76000** a year until the age of 87 (including a part Age Pension), or **$62000** a year until the age of 100 (including a part Age Pension).

By doing nothing, Sal and Vladimir are three-quarters of the way towards their retirement target of **$100000** a year.

Doing a little delivers Sal and Vladimir $100000 a year, until age 87

By using a salary sacrifice strategy, Sal and Vladimir can substantially boost their super savings while reducing their income tax bill. By each contributing $5000 of before-tax salary to a superannuation account through salary sacrifice, they will have an immediate net tax benefit of $1500 ($750 each) because they pay 15 per cent tax on the super contributions, rather than 30 per cent tax (for 2011–12) on non-super income. From 2012–13 (subject to the legislation being passed), the couple will get a combined $1750 bonus ($875 each) each year towards their superannuation balances by paying 15 per cent tax on super contributions rather than 32.5 per cent on non-super income (see chapter 10 for more information on salary sacrifice).

By salary sacrificing $5000 each, every year, the couple can expect the following outcomes:

- Sal can expect a final retirement balance at age 67 of **$669 000**.

- Vladimir can expect a final retirement balance at age 67 of **$785 000**.

- The couple will then have a combined final retirement balance of **$1 454 000** at age 67.

Assuming no Age Pension, by starting superannuation pensions (income streams) with **$1 454 000** at age 67, Sal and Vladimir can expect to receive **$100 000** a year until the age of 87, or **$77 000** a year until the age of 100 (see table 9.4). Not bad for just a little effort!

Table 9.4: Sal and Vladimir's super balance if they do nothing, a little, a lot or heaps (Sal is aged 35, has a $20 000 starting account balance and earns $70 000 a year; Vladimir is aged 35, has a $40 000 starting account balance, and earns $80 000 a year)

Sal and Vladimir (age 35)	Combined retirement balances at age 67 $	Annual tax-free retirement income (from age 67)	
Super contributions		Until age 87 $	Until age 100 $
Doing nothing			
SG only	921 000*	64 000/**76 000**	48 000/**62 000**
Concessional (before-tax) contributions			
Doing a little			
SG + $5000 a year (salary sacrifice)	1 454 000	100 000	77 000
Doing a lot			
SG + $7500 a year (salary sacrifice)	1 586 000	110 000	84 000
Doing heaps			
SG + $10 000 a year (salary sacrifice)	1 720 000	120 000	91 000

* With this lump sum amount, a generous part Age Pension is possible, and if they are eligible for the Age Pension, the annual income will be that shown as the second amount in the third and fourth columns of the table. With other lump sum amounts in table 9.4, a part Age Pension is not available on retirement, but may be available in the later years of retirement. For other table assumptions see the appendix.

Doing heaps delivers Sal and Vladimir $100 000 a year, until age 94

If the couple want to do a lot, they could consider the following strategies:

- *Vladimir salary sacrifices $7500 a year (doing a lot)*. Vladimir's final retirement balance could then be **$917 000,** giving the couple a combined final retirement balance of **$1 586 000 ($669 000 + $917 000).** Assuming no Age Pension, this impressive balance of **$1.586 million** can give the couple **$110 000** a year income, tax-free, until the age of 87, or **$84 000** a year until the age of 100 (see table 9.4 on p. 135), or **$100 000** a year until the age of 91. If Vladimir opts for this more aggressive strategy (making his own before-tax contributions of about $145 each week), he can reduce his annual income tax bill by $2250 (for 2011–12) or $2437 from 2012–13 (subject to the legislation being passed). His super contributions will be subject to 15 per cent tax in the super fund, giving him an annual net tax benefit of $1125 (for 2011–12, or $1312 from 2012–13).

- *Vladimir salary sacrifices $10 000 a year (doing heaps)*. Vladimir's final retirement balance could then be **$1 051 000,** giving the couple a combined final retirement balance of **$1 720 000** at age 67 (see table 9.4). Assuming no Age Pension, the lump sum amount of **$1 720 000** can deliver the couple an annual retirement income of **$120 000** a year until the age of 87, or **$91 000** a year until the age of 100, or **$100 000** a year until the age of 94. By making these contributions (about $195 each week), Vladimir also reduces his annual income tax bill by $3000 (for 2011–12, and $3250 from 2012–13, subject to the legislation being passed), although his super contributions are subject to 15 per cent tax ($1500) within the fund.

Sal is excited about their financial position and proud that she had a go at the Six-Step Wealth Check. The couple are cruising into retirement, and Sal is confident that they will build enough savings to deliver a tax-free retirement income of **$100 000** a year until the age of 100 (**$1.9 million**) (see table 9.3 on p. 133). Sal intends to redirect more of her salary to her super account once their children have reached university age.

Now that she has done some of her cost-of-living calculations, she is wondering whether they will really need $100 000 a year in retirement.

If Sal gets a divorce, can she create a $60 000 a year retirement on her own?

If Sal's marriage breaks down before she retires, what can she expect in retirement if she has to rely on her own superannuation savings? She can expect a very comfortable retirement if she implements her proposed savings plan. For simplicity, assume Vladimir and Sal agreed not to split superannuation savings on divorce, and they each retained their own super savings and divvied up other assets.

Sal is keen to secure the **$60 000** a year tax-free income in retirement that she believes will enable her to create a wonderful life for herself in retirement. If she retires at age 67, she will need at least **$860 000** on retirement, assuming no Age Pension (see table 9.3 on p. 133). If she takes into account a part Age Pension that she is likely to receive in the later years of retirement, then she will need only **$802 000** to reach her dream retirement income (see table 9.5 on p. 139).

Sal considers different super strategies: doing nothing (SG only), a little, a lot or doing heaps. She is excited to learn that if she makes $7500 in concessional contributions (through salary sacrifice) each year, in addition to her employer's compulsory super contributions, she can expect her **$60 000** a year tax-free retirement (assuming part Age Pension) to last until age 87. If she wants this level of income until age 100, then she can consider redirecting additional money to super when she is in her fifties.

> **Tip**
>
> The next section, detailing Sal's super strategies if she retires as a single woman, is fairly busy with figures. A quick cuppa may be in order if you need a brain break.

If Sal retires at age 67 (see table 9.5 on p. 139), she can expect the following outcomes:

- *Doing nothing (SG only) delivers $41 000 a year.* Sal's final retirement balance of **$403 000** can deliver **$41 000** a year until the age of 87 (including a part Age Pension), which is more than a comfortable lifestyle for a single person. If Sal wants her savings to last until she reaches the age of 100, then the **$403 000** retirement balance can deliver **$35 000** a year (including a part Age Pension) (see table 9.5).

- *Doing a little (SG + $5000 salary sacrifice) delivers $54 000 a year.* By making $5000 in before-tax (concessional) contributions each year, on top of her employer's compulsory SG contributions, Sal can expect to retire with a final account balance of **$669 000**. A final balance of **$669 000** can deliver Sal **$46 000** a year until the age of 87, or **$35 000** a year until the age of 100 years, assuming she gets no Age Pension (see table 9.5). Sal can, however, expect a part Age Pension very early into her retirement, which means her lump sum can deliver around **$54 000** until the age of 87 (including part Age Pension from age 68) or **$43 000** until the age of 100 (including a part Age Pension from age 69).

- *Doing a lot (SG + $7500 salary sacrifice), delivers $60 000 a year.* By making $7500 in salary sacrificed contributions in addition to her employer's SG contributions, Sal can retire at age 67 with an account balance of **$802 000**, delivering **$56 000** until age 87, or **$42 000** until age 100, assuming no Age Pension. If she takes into account her Age Pension entitlements taking effect a few years after retiring, then Sal's lump sum of **$802 000** will deliver **$60 000** until age 87 (including a part Age Pension from age 72), or **$47 000** a year until age 100 (including a part Age Pension from age 72 — see table 9.5). Sal's savings plan can deliver her the dream retirement target of **$60 000** a year, to the age of 87.

- *Doing heaps (SG +$7500 salary sacrifice to 55 + $12 000 salary sacrifice from 55 to 67) delivers $60 000 a year, until age 90.* Sal has achieved her dream retirement figure of **$60 000** a year in retirement, until the age of 87. If she wants this level of income to last beyond the age of 87, then she may have to increase her super contributions later on in life. If she ramps up her contributions later in life, say, from age 55 to 67, she will extend this level of retirement income for a few more years. From the age of 55 to age 67, if Sal makes salary sacrifice contributions of **$12 000** a year (that is, $1000 a month, or $250 a week) she can expect a final retirement balance of **$860 000**, which can deliver her an income of **$60 000** a year until age 90 (including a part Age Pension from the age of 74). Alternatively, her lump sum can deliver her **$63 000** until age 87 (including part Age Pension from age 74), or **$50 000** a year until age 100 (including a part Age Pension from the age of 78 — see table 9.5).

Table 9.5: Sal's super balance and retirement income if she does nothing, a little, a lot, or heaps (age 35, starting balance $20000, income $70000 a year)

Sal (age 35)	Retirement balance at age 67 $	Annual tax-free retirement income			
		Until age 87		Until age 100	
Super contributions		No Age Pension $	Part Age Pension $	No Age Pension $	Part Age Pension $
Doing nothing					
SG only	403 000	28 000	**41 000**	21 000	**35 000**
Concessional (before-tax) contributions					
Doing a little					
SG +$5000 a year (salary sacrifice)	669 000	46 000	**54 000**	35 000	**43 000**
Doing a lot					
SG + $7500 a year (salary sacrifice)	802 000	56 000	**60 000**	42 000	**47 000**
Doing heaps					
SG + $7500 until 55 + $12 000 from 55 to 67	860 000	60 000	**63 000**	45 000	**50 000**

Note: A single person retiring with a lump sum amount listed in table 9.5 is likely to receive a part Age Pension at some stage in their retirement. For table assumptions see the appendix.

Case study 3 (age 45): Maree learns lots about long-term saving

Maree is 45 years of age and keen to accumulate savings for her retirement. She wants to retire on $60 000 a year when she turns 65, but discovers that she can't claim the Age Pension until she is 67. Maree received an inheritance from her mother's estate recently, and used the inheritance to make a non-concessional (after-tax) contribution to her super account.

She now has $110 000 in super. Apart from that large contribution, Maree hasn't had a chance to accumulate superannuation because she has been raising her children and working part-time as a self-employed consultant in human resources. Maree is divorced, and although she was entitled to claim on her husband's super benefits, the couple made a private agreement that Maree would receive the house with a small mortgage outstanding and a lump sum, and her ex-husband would receive his super benefits. Her lawyers advised her to claim on her husband's super, but Maree didn't want to move the kids, and wanted a stress-free mortgage.

Maree has now paid off her mortgage. She has started a full-time job in human resources earning $120 000 a year (plus super), and knows that she has to start making serious plans for retirement.

Maree considers the following scenarios:

- If Maree wants to retire on an income of **$60 000** a year in retirement from the age of 67, then she will need to plan for a retirement savings target of **$860 000** (for this level of income to last until she turns 87), or **$1.14 million** (for this level of income to last until she turns 100), assuming no Age Pension.

- If Maree wants to retire at age 65, on **$60 000** a year, then her retirement savings target will range between **$910 000** (lasting until age 87) and **$1.17 million** (lasting until age 100), assuming no Age Pension (see table 9.6).

Maree is likely to be eligible for a part Age Pension at some stage during her retirement, which means the lump sum amount that she will need to finance **$60 000** a year until the age of 87, or until the age of 100, may be a lot less than the amounts listed in table 9.6. Continue reading to find out more.

Table 9.6: how much money is enough? Maree is aged 45 and wants a retirement income of $60 000 a year without any Age Pension

Maree's target retirement income $	Retiring at 60, and money lasts until: $		Retiring at 65, and money lasts until: $		Retiring at 67, and money lasts until: $	
	Age 87 $	Age 100 $	Age 87 $	Age 100 $	Age 87 $	Age 100 $
60 000	1.02 m	1.23 m	910 000	1.17 m	860 000	1.14 m

Note: For table assumptions see the appendix.

Doing nothing (SG only) gives Maree $48 000 a year in retirement

Maree can expect these outcomes if she does nothing but turn up for work:

- *Retire at 67.* If Maree works until she is 67 years of age, that is, for the next 22 years, and relies only on her employer's compulsory contributions (SG), then her final account balance is likely to be **$570 000**. If Maree does nothing else towards her retirement plans, and commences a superannuation pension with her final account balance, she can expect an annual income of **$48 000** (including a part Age Pension) until age 87, or **$40 000** (including a part Age Pension) until the age of 100. If Maree is not eligible for the Age Pension (see chapter 11) when she retires at age 67, her **$570 000** would deliver **$37 000** a year (until the age of 87) or **$29 000** a year (until the age of 100). (See table 9.7.)

- *Retire at 65.* If Maree chooses to retire at age 65, then she won't be eligible for the Age Pension for two years and will have to wholly rely on her own savings before claiming a part Age Pension from the age of 67. If Maree chooses to retire at age 65, then her retirement account balance will be **$511 000**, and she can expect an annual income of **$43 000** (until age 87, having no access to a part Age Pension for the first two years) or **$36 000** (until age 100, having no access to an Age Pension for the first two years). If for some reason Maree is not eligible for the Age Pension after the first two years of retirement, her **$511 000** at age 65 would deliver **$33 000** (until age 87) or **$26 000** (until age 100). (See table 9.8 on p. 144.)

Maree is very excited about her retirement prospects. Without doing much at all, she can already expect to receive 80 per cent (**$48 000**) of her target of **$60 000**. Maree is now motivated to create her ideal retirement lifestyle.

Table 9.7: Maree's super balance and retirement income if she does nothing, a little or a lot, and retires at 67 (age 45, starting balance $110 000, income $120 000 a year)

Maree (age 45) Super contributions	Retirement balance at age 67 $	Annual tax-free retirement income from age 67			
		Until age 87		Until age 100	
		No Age Pension $	Part Age Pension $	No Age Pension $	Part Age Pension $
Doing nothing					
SG only	570 000	37 000	48 000	29 000	40 000
Concessional (before-tax) contributions					
Doing a little					
SG + $5000 a year (salary sacrifice	717 000	49 500	56 000	37 500	44 500
Doing a lot					
SG +$12 000 a year (salary sacrifice)	910 000	63 000	66 000	47 000	52 000

Note: For table assumptions see the appendix.

Doing a little delivers Maree $56000 a year in retirement

By making $5000 in before-tax (concessional) contributions each year (about $96 a week), in addition to her employer's SG contributions, Maree can expect to retire with a final account balance of **$717000** at age 67, or **$638000** at age 65.

By doing a little, Maree can expect the following outcomes:

- *Retire at 67.* Her final account balance of **$717000** can deliver Maree an annual retirement income of **$56000** until the age of 87 (including part Age Pension from age 70), or **$44500** until the age of 100 (including part Age Pension from age 71). If Maree is not eligible for the Age Pension (see chapter 11) when she retires at age 67, her **$717000** would deliver **$49500** a year (until the age of 87) or **$37500** a year (until the age of 100). (See table 9.7 on p. 141.)

- *Retire at 65.* Maree's final account balance of **$638000** can deliver an annual retirement income of around **$50000** (until age 87, having no access to a part Age Pension for the first two years) and around **$41000** (until age 100, having no access to the Age Pension for the first two years). If for some reason Maree is not eligible for the Age Pension after the first two years of retirement, her **$638000** at age 65 would deliver around **$42000** a year (until age 87) or about **$32500** a year (until age 100). (See table 9.8 on p. 144.)

Maree is very close to her target retirement income of **$60000** a year when retiring at age 67. She believes she can spare a few more dollars each year to put towards her retirement plans.

Doing a lot delivers Maree $60000 a year in retirement, until age 91

Maree intends to make substantial concessional (before-tax) contributions to her super account, through salary sacrifice. She can make up to $25000 each year in concessional contributions (for 2011–12; see chapter 10), but this $25000 contributions cap includes her employer's annual SG contributions of $10800. Maree decides to contribute **$12000** a year (about $230 a week) as concessional contributions, which saves her $4200 in income tax each year (although her super contributions are subject to a contributions tax of $1800). In short, her after-tax income has been reduced by only $7560 for the year (or about $145 a week) rather than $12 000 ($230 a week), while her super account has received a substantial boost. Her concessional contributions (including SG) now total **$22 800** each year.

Relying on her doing a lot strategy, Maree can expect the following outcomes:

- *Retire at 67*. Maree can expect to have a final retirement balance of **$910 000**. This lump sum amount at age 67 can deliver Maree **$66 000** until the age of 87 (including part Age Pension from the age of 75), or **$52 000** a year until the age of 100 (including a part Age Pension from the age of 80). If Maree is not eligible for the Age Pension (see chapter 11) when she retires at age 67, her **$910 000** could deliver around **$63 000** a year (until the age of 87) or just under **$47 000** a year (until the age of 100). (See table 9.7 on p. 141.) From the age of 67, if Maree lives on **$60 000** a year, as she desires, **$910 000** will deliver that level of income (a combination of super and Age Pension) until the age of 91. Not bad at all! Beyond that age, Maree can expect to rely solely on the Age Pension.

- *Retire at 65*. Maree can expect to have a final retirement balance of **$806 000** by relying on her doing a lot strategy. This lump sum amount at age 65 can deliver Maree **$57 000** until the age of 87 (including a part Age Pension from the age of 71), or **$46 000** a year until the age of 100 (including a part Age Pension from the age of 74). If Maree is not eligible for the Age Pension when she retires at age 65, her **$806 000** in today's dollars could deliver around **$53 000** a year (until the age of 87) or **$41 000** a year (until the age of 100). (See table 9.8 overleaf.)

Maree easily meets her dream target of **$60 000** a year in retirement by contributing $1000 a month ($12 000 a year) as salary sacrifice contributions. If Maree wants **$60 000** a year until the age of 100, rather than until the age of 91, then she will need about **$1.14 million** at age 67. Retiring with this much money as a single person means she can expect a minimal Age Pension, and any Age Pension entitlements will only become available in the later years of her retirement.

If Maree wants to retire on **$60 000** a year in today's dollars from the age of 65, and for that income to last until the age of 100, then she needs to plan for a retirement savings target of **$1.17 million** (see table 9.6 on p. 140). She can choose several strategies to make this happen, including increasing her contributions further as Maree gets closer to retirement (see chapter 10).

Table 9.8: Maree's super balance and retirement income if she does nothing, a little or a lot, and retires at 65 (age 45, starting balance $110 000, income $120 000 a year)

Maree (age 45)	Retirement balance at age 65 $	Annual tax-free retirement income from age 65			
		Until age 87		Until age 100	
Super contributions		No Age Pension $	Part Age Pension $	No Age Pension $	Part Age Pension $
Doing nothing					
SG only	511 000	33 000	**43 000**	26 000	**36 000**
Concessional (before-tax) contributions					
Doing a little					
SG + $5000 a year (salary sacrifice	638 000	42 000	**50 000**	32 500	**41 000**
Doing a lot					
SG +$12 000 a year (salary sacrifice)	806 000	53 000	**57 000**	41 000	**46 000**

Note: For table assumptions see the appendix.

Case study 4 (age 55): Julianne's jolly glad good things come to those who plan

Julianne is 55, and intends to retire at age 65. She wants the same lifestyle in retirement that she enjoys today, while she is working. This lifestyle enables her to go out for dinner two or three times a week, head overseas every year, improve her golf handicap as a member of a private golf club, and host regular dinners at home. Julianne has worked out that she probably needs about $60 000 a year, especially since she is helping out one of her daughters financially who is bringing up three children on her own.

Julianne's husband passed away three years ago, and she used his life insurance payout to pay off the house, and the balance of the payout she contributed to her super fund as a non-concessional (after-tax) contribution. She has $500 000 in her superannuation account, and works for herself as an IT consultant. She earns $90 000 a year in her own business. She runs her business as a company, which therefore means she must pay compulsory employer contributions (SG) of $8100 on her own behalf.

If Julianne wants to retire on an income of **$60 000** from the age of 65, then she will need to plan for a retirement savings target of **$910 000** (for this level of income to last until she turns 87), or **$1.17 million** (to last until she turns 100), assuming no Age Pension (see table 9.9).

Julianne wants some cushioning because she expects to live a long life like her parents—her Dad died at the age of 95 last year, and her mother is aged 87 and still enjoys reasonable health. Julianne believes **$1.17 million** will give her a safety net, even though she doesn't plan to be alive at the age of 100. If she has any money left, her kids can have it.

In short, Julianne wants to more than double her superannuation savings within 10 years. Can she do it?

If Julianne decides to delay her retirement until age 67, then she will need **$860 000** (to provide **$60 000** a year until age 87), or **$1.14 million** until age 100, assuming no Age Pension (see table 9.9).

Julianne is likely to be eligible for a part Age Pension at some stage during her retirement, which means the lump sum amount that she needs to finance **$60 000** a year until the age of 87, or until the age of 100, may be a lot smaller than the lump sums listed in table 9.9. Continue reading to find out more about Julianne's plans.

Table 9.9: how much money is enough? Julianne is aged 55 and wants a retirement income of $60 000 a year, with no Age Pension

Julianne's target retirement income $	Retiring at 60, and money lasts until:		Retiring at 65, and money lasts until:		Retiring at 67, and money lasts until	
	Age 87 $	Age 100 $	Age 87 $	Age 100 $	Age 87 $	Age 100 $
60 000	1.02 m	1.23 m	10 000	1.17 m	860 000	1.14 m

Note: For table assumptions see the appendix.

Doing nothing (SG only) gives Julianne $57 000 a year in retirement

If Julianne works until she is 65 years of age, that is, for the next 10 years, and relies only on her employer's compulsory contributions (SG) of **$8100** each year, then her final account balance is likely to be **$816 000** in today's dollars.

If Julianne decides to opt for a do nothing strategy, her final account balance can deliver an income of nearly **$58 000** until the age of 87 (including a small part Age Pension from the age of 71), or **$46 000** until the age of 100 (including a part Age Pension from the age of 75—see table 9.10 on p. 147). This low-key strategy is within a cat's whisker of delivering Julianne's retirement dream. Not bad!

If, for some reason, Julianne isn't able to claim the Age Pension (see chapter 11) in her later years, then at age 65 her retirement balance of $816 000 can deliver **$54 000** until the age of 87, or **$42 000** until the age of 100 (see table 9.10). Again, not bad at all!

Doing a little delivers Julianne around $60 000 in retirement, until age 87

By using a salary sacrifice strategy, Julianne can substantially boost her super savings while reducing her income tax. By contributing $5000 of before-tax salary to her super account, Julianne enjoys an immediate net tax benefit of $1100 because she pays 15 per cent tax on the super contributions, rather than 37 per cent tax on income (see the appendix for income tax rates). In effect, Julianne gets a $1100 bonus boost each year towards her superannuation.

By salary sacrificing $5000 each year (about $96 a week), for the next 10 years, Julianne can expect a final retirement balance of **$867 000** in today's dollars, which can deliver **$60 000** until the age of 87 (including a small part Age Pension from the age of 72), which is bang on her dream target of **$60 000** a year for her retirement. If Julianne wants her money to last until she reaches the age of 100, then she can expect **$867 000** to deliver **$48 000** a year (including a small part Age Pension from the age of 72 — see table 9.10).

If Julianne is not eligible for the Age Pension (see chapter 11) in her seventies, then her lump sum of **$867 000** will deliver **$56 500** until she turns 87, or **$44 000** until the age of 100.

Julianne is relieved that she can achieve her retirement dream of **$60 000** a year with very little effort or sacrifice. Julianne wants her retirement dream to last beyond the age of 87 years, so she is willing to consider making larger super contributions.

Doing a lot delivers Julianne $63 000 a year in retirement

Julianne intends to make substantial concessional (before-tax) contributions to her super account, through salary sacrifice. She decides to contribute **$10 000** a year (about $190 a week) as concessional contributions, which saves her $3700 in income tax each year (although her super contributions are subject to a contributions tax of $1500). In short, her after-tax income has been reduced by only $6300 for the year (or $121 a week) rather than $10 000 ($190 a week), while her super account has received a substantial boost. Her concessional contributions (including SG) now total **$18 100** each year.

If Julianne follows this strategy, her final retirement balance will be **$919 000**, which can deliver **$63 000** a year until the age of 87 (including a small part Age Pension from the age of 74), or **$60 000** until the age of 89, or **$50 000** a year until she turns 100 (including a small part Age Pension from the age of 79 — see table 9.10).

If Julianne doesn't claim the Age Pension when she is eligible, her **$919 000** account balance can still deliver her **$60 000** a year in retirement until the age of 87, or **$47 000** a year until the age of 100 (see table 9.10).

Julianne is very excited about these figures. She knows that closer to her retirement date she can make some further contributions to boost her super account to the desired target of **$1.17 million,** to deliver her $60 000 a year until the age of 100. She may even decide to work part time for part of her retirement, which means she will need fewer savings to finance her lifestyle.

Table 9.10: Julianne's super balance and retirement income if she does nothing, a little, or a lot, and retiring at 65 (age 55, starting balance $500 000, income $90 000 a year

Julianne (age 55)	Retirement balance at age 65 $	Annual tax-free retirement income from age 65			
		Until age 87		Until age 100	
Super contributions		No Age Pension $	Part Age Pension $	No Age Pension $	Part Age Pension $
Doing nothing					
SG only	816 000	54 000	**58 000**	42 000	**46 000**
Concessional (after-tax) contributions					
Doing a little					
SG +$5000 a year (salary sacrifice)	867 000	56 500	**60 000**	44 000	**48 000**
Doing a lot					
SG + $10 000 salary sacrifice	919 000	60 000	**63 000**	47 000	**50 000**

Note: For table assumptions see the appendix.

Part III

The good life beckons—a few more important things to think about

Chapter 10

Boost your super: 15 tips to help you create a worry-free financial future

" *Too much of a good thing can be wonderful.* "

Mae West, American actress

If you want a worry-free financial future then you need to think about what this future is going to look like. After taking my Six-Step Wealth Check, you may have decided there's a financial gap between what you want and what your superannuation and non-superannuation savings are going to deliver if you continue on your current path.

In terms of superannuation, you have numerous choices to help you close this financial gap including choosing a super fund that offers lower fees, making voluntary super contributions, reducing the taxes that you pay by using super strategies, taking more investment risk, delaying retirement, and even continuing to work and contributing to super after you have retired.

This chapter offers 15 tips to help you boost your super savings. I have divided the 15 tips into three parts so, if you wish, you can approach your possible super-boosting plan in three stages:

- super quick fixes that can save you thousands of dollars (tips 1 to 5)

- simple, and free, super strategies that can help you build a larger nest egg (tips 6 to 10)

- strategies to rev up your super balance in a major way (tips 11 to 15).

As a handy reference, I have included a one-page checklist of the 15 tips on page 173.

If you want more information

The 15 tips in this chapter are a summary of the key features of some of the easiest and most popular superannuation strategies. For more detailed information about the super rules and how they work, and the latest super rates and thresholds, visit my free consumer website, SuperGuide at <www.superguide.com.au>.

Super quick fixes can save thousands of dollars

You can start with picking what I call the low-hanging fruit—the strategies that are quick, save you money immediately, and cost nothing to implement:

- *Tip 1:* Give your tax file number (TFN) to your super fund, so you won't pay unnecessary tax.

- *Tip 2:* Find out how many super funds you have, and update your contact details.

- *Tip 3:* Consider combining your super accounts, to reduce how much you pay in fees.

- *Tip 4:* Check that your employer is making compulsory employer contributions (SG) for you, and that the contribution amount is correct.

- *Tip 5:* Check your life insurance cover in your super fund.

Tip 1: Give your tax file number (TFN) to your super fund, so you won't pay unnecessary tax

The easiest first step you can take to help along your superannuation savings is to check that your super fund has your tax file number (TFN). If your super fund doesn't have your TFN recorded for your super account, you can expect the following consequences:

- Your employer's compulsory super contributions (SG) are hit with penalty tax of 31.5 per cent, in addition to the usual 15 per cent contributions tax — that's a whopping 46.5 per cent tax on what is supposed to be a tax-friendly savings plan.

- If you have made your own concessional (before-tax) contributions, then those super contributions will also be hit with 31.5 per cent penalty tax, in addition to the 15 per cent contributions tax; taking the total to 46.5 per cent of the super contribution. Now, that's not nice. (See tip 11 for information on concessional contributions.)

- You won't be able to make any non-concessional (after-tax) contributions to your super fund. (See tip 12 for information on non-concessional contributions.)

- If you can't make non-concessional contributions, then you won't have access to the co-contribution scheme. (See tip 13 for information on co-contributions.)

Tip 2: Find out how many super funds you have, and update your contact details

The average Australian of working age has around three superannuation accounts scattered throughout the super system, although some people may have many more super accounts.

You're likely to have more than one super account if you have worked part time at a series of jobs while at school or at university, or while rearing children, or just because you've had a lot of part-time or casual jobs. You might not even know that your employer was making compulsory super contributions for you while you were working in a casual job. If you have changed full-time jobs regularly, you may also have more than one super account.

Do you know the name of your super fund?

Do you know the names of each of your superannuation funds, and do you have a record of your member account number for each super fund?

You could be one of those rare individuals who ensures that your superannuation fund knows your new address when you move house, which means you would have received regular member reports from each of your super funds. One more question: did you keep those statements?

If you haven't kept the paperwork from your super funds, but you know what super funds that you belong to, then recording your member details is a straightforward process. Contact each super fund and ask for this information, and then confirm that your personal details for each account (including contact details) are correct. You will have to prove your identity to the super fund, for example by providing your date of birth and possibly other key information. While you're doing this bit of super housekeeping, check out your current account balance for each super account (see tip 6 for more information on conducting a financial stocktake of your super savings).

If you don't know the name of your super fund

If you don't know the names of your super funds, or you don't know how many super accounts that you have out there in super land, then you may have to do a little more work; but not much more. You can find your super accounts by using one or more of the following free services:

- *SuperSeeker.* The Australian Tax Office (ATO) provides a location service for super accounts called SuperSeeker. The service searches special databases including the Lost Members Register and the Unclaimed Super Register. You can access the service by visiting the ATO superannuation website at <www.ato.gov.au> or by phoning the ATO on 13 28 65. At a minimum, you will need to provide your tax file number and date of birth to get access to the SuperSeeker service.

- *AUSfund.* The AUSfund super fund looks after the lost super accounts that have been transferred from some of the largest super funds in Australia. You can visit the AUSfund website at <www.unclaimedsuper.com.au>.

- *Approach your current super fund.* Ask your super fund if they offer a service to locate your lost super. If you intend to transfer other super accounts into an account with your current super fund, you will probably find your current super fund will be very helpful in locating and transferring your stray accounts.

- *Contact your previous employers.* You can ask previous employers for the names of the super fund(s) they used when paying your compulsory employer contributions (SG). (See chapter 6.)

Tip 3: Consider combining your super accounts, to reduce how much you pay in fees

By reducing or removing unnecessary costs, you can add a quick few thousand dollars to your super savings over time. You can cut the amount of fees that you pay instantly by combining superannuation accounts if you have more than one. Many super funds charge a flat administration fee that you pay regardless of the size of your account. If you have more than one account, you're paying this fee more than once — over a working life these extra fees can add up to thousands of dollars.

Since most super funds offer life and permanent disability insurance to members, the cost of which is deducted from your super account, you may also find that you're paying insurance premiums for more than one policy, when you may not necessarily need this level of cover (see tip 5). If you're paying insurance premiums in more than one super fund, and you don't need this much insurance or worse, you don't know that you have this insurance, then that's a few more thousand dollars missing from your super fund on retirement.

If you die while a member of a super fund, you can generally expect insurance companies to pay death benefits on each of the life insurance policies. But if you make a disability claim on more than one permanent disability policy or on more than one income protection policy taken out through your super funds, it's unlikely that each policy will pay you on your one claim. If you're concerned about the extent of your insurance cover, or your position where you have multiple policies, then contact your super fund.

Once you have located your superannuation accounts (see tip 2), you can then transfer the account balances into one super fund account (see tip 7 for information about how to review or choose a super fund). Your current super fund may help you when transferring account balances from other super funds to your current fund. In some cases it may not be possible to transfer an account balance, or not financially worthwhile to transfer because of exit fees payable on some super accounts.

Ask your super fund for an estimate of any fees (including withdrawal fees) that will be payable, or any benefits that will be lost, for transferring money out of a super fund.

Tip 4: Check that your employer is making compulsory super contributions (SG) for you and that the contribution amount is correct

Under the SG rules, if you're an eligible employee, your employer is currently required to pay the equivalent of 9 per cent of your annual salary to a superannuation account, on your behalf. Your employer's contributions must be paid at least quarterly, and sometimes monthly, depending on the rules of the super fund accepting the super contributions.

Hopefully, you already know how much money is going into your super account each year, but if you don't, you can ask your employer, and find out whether the payments are made quarterly, monthly or fortnightly. You can then check whether this amount equals 9 per cent of your salary, and you can check with your super fund whether your fund has received this money. (See chapter 6 for more information on SG and how to check up on your employer.)

Employer must pay your contributions within 28 days

If you make after-tax (non-concessional) contributions to a super fund and you make these payments by a deduction from your salary (arranged with your employer), then your employer is required to direct these payments to your super fund within 28 days of the end of the month in which the amount was deducted from your salary. This means, for example, that your employer deducts an amount on 15 March, representing your after-tax contribution for your super fund, but legally does not have to pay that amount into your super fund until 28 April.

Tip 5: Check your life insurance cover in your super fund

You're likely to be paying life insurance premiums through your superannuation fund account. Most super funds automatically deduct premiums for life insurance (also known as death cover), and this cover often includes permanent disability cover, to provide you with a lump sum or income stream in the event that you're permanently disabled and you can no longer work. If you have more than one super account, then you may be paying for the same cover more than once, which may not make financial sense.

It's a good idea to work out how much life insurance cover you need, and then ensure the cover that you pay for through your super fund will meet your needs, or your family's needs, if a claim is made on the insurance policy. Tip 3 explains what may happen if you have to make a claim and you hold more than one insurance policy.

Some super funds also automatically deduct premiums for income protection insurance, which will pay you part of your regular income if you have an accident or suffer illness that temporarily prevents you from working.

A super fund can provide cost-effective insurance cover for you or your family, but the minimum coverage automatically provided by most super funds may not be sufficient to look after your family if you do fall ill or die. I explain your insurance options with super funds, and some of the other steps you can take to look after yourself or your family if you fall ill or die, on my free consumer website, SuperGuide at <www.superguide.com.au>.

Simple, and free, super strategies for building a larger nest egg

Tips 6 to 10 are strategies that take a bit more energy, but still don't have to cost you anything to implement, or don't require you to make any radical changes — except, perhaps, if you decide to change super funds or change investment options. The simple and free super strategies are:

- *Tip 6:* Do a financial stocktake for today and for tomorrow.

- *Tip 7:* Review your fund — is your super fund good enough for your retirement plans?

- *Tip 8:* Check your super fund's investment returns.

- *Tip 9:* Review your investment option, and change investment options, if necessary.

- *Tip 10:* Identify your dependants and non-dependants.

Tip 6: Do a financial stocktake for today and for tomorrow

A financial stocktake involves answering the following questions:

- How much money do you have in your super account today?

- What's the total of your other savings and investments, if any?

- What will your current super and non-super savings, and current strategies (if any) deliver for you when you retire?

Working out what your starting point is when creating a brighter financial future can be liberating. You draw a line in the sand today, and you then estimate what your current strategies will give you tomorrow in terms of a lump sum.

Start with a stocktake of your superannuation savings. In other words, follow steps 4 and 5 of my Six-Step Wealth Check (see chapter 4).

If you keep the member statements that your super fund sends you, at least once a year, then doing a financial stocktake of your current super savings is a piece of cake. Ensuring that your super fund (or funds) has your current contact details will ensure that you receive your super fund member statements (see tip 2).

Your regular super fund member statements give you a good start for conducting a regular financial stocktake. You can also contact your super fund by telephone or email to check your super account balance, or log onto your super fund's special members only website to access your account information, if your fund offers this service and you have registered for it (see tip 2). Many super funds update member accounts monthly, weekly or even daily.

Once you have worked out how much you have in your super account, or super accounts, you can work out what those savings will deliver at some future point in time (retirement age) if you continue what you're doing now (which may be doing nothing). Your super fund may provide an online calculator that you can use to work out this amount, or you can use the free MoneySmart superannuation calculator, maintained by ASIC. I use the ASIC MoneySmart calculators throughout this book.

You can then work out whether there is a gap between what you will have in savings when you retire if you continue your current strategies, and what you need for the life that you imagine. My Six-Step Wealth Check helps you work out the:

- lifestyle you want in retirement (step 1)

- cost of your chosen lifestyle (step 2)

- lump sum you need on retirement to deliver your chosen lifestyle (step 3).

(See chapter 4 for the entire Six-Step Wealth Check process.)

Tip 7: Review your fund — is your super fund good enough for your retirement plans?

Although most Australians can now choose their own super fund, most Aussies remain in the super fund their employer chooses. The common triggers for Australian women to check the merits of their current superannuation fund include the following:

- *Change of employment.* When changing jobs, if you have the right to choose your own super fund, your new employer will give you a Standard Choice Form. You use this form to indicate what super fund you want your employer to pay your compulsory superannuation contributions (SG) into. If you don't complete the form, your employer's contributions will be paid into a default super fund, usually chosen by the employer, although sometimes specified in an industrial award.

- *Poor investment performance.* If your super fund performs poorly, it's a natural reaction to want to find out whether the low returns (or even investment losses) were the result of bad investment decisions by your super fund, or poorly performing investment markets. If your super fund's returns are similar to the investment returns delivered by the majority of other super funds investing in similar assets (see tip 8), then it's likely the investment markets are mainly to blame for the poor performance. You can find out about your super fund's investment performance on your fund's website, or refer to your most recent annual member statement (if you still have it handy). If you don't like the returns your super account is delivering, you may want to reconsider your super account's investment option (see tip 9), or you could change your super fund.

- *High super fund fees.* A super fund that charges considerably more than 1 per cent of your account balance in annual fees can be considered a high fee fund. High fees can eat into long-term investment returns. According to the government consumer website, MoneySmart, a 1 per cent difference in fees can mean a 20 per cent smaller retirement balance after 30 years. For example, if your super fund, Fund A, charges 2 per cent in total fees while Fund B charges 1 per cent in fees, then you can expect your final retirement balance to be 20 per cent smaller in Fund A compared with what your super saving could have been if you had chosen Fund B (assuming investment returns were identical in both super funds).

High fees can be a compelling reason to change super funds unless you choose that super fund for other reasons: for example, a more expensive super fund may be chosen for better life insurance coverage or for the ability to invest in assets not available in your current super fund, or for access to more sophisticated reporting and account monitoring tools.

- *Combining super funds.* If you're considering combining one or more of your super accounts, you have to decide which super fund will be your preferred super fund; that is, the super fund that will receive the account balances from your other super accounts.

What to consider when reviewing your super fund

A super fund's investment performance and level of fees are the most important factors when considering the merits of a super fund, although insurance cover can be important too. You can rate your super fund, and other funds, against criteria such as long-term investment performance; the number of investment options offered; fees charged; types of insurance available and what it costs; and extra services, such as financial planning services and cheaper home loans.

Is it time to change super funds?

If you can find a super fund that delivers you better long-term performance than your current fund, and this alternative super fund charges reasonable fees and also offers cost-effective insurance, then changing super funds may be a worthwhile option (visit SuperGuide at <www.superguide.com.au> for more information on choosing a super fund).

Tip 8: Check your super fund's investment returns

Do you know your super fund account's investment performance over one year, three years, five years, seven years and 10 years? If you don't know, then you have some homework to do. No need to worry—finding out your super fund's long-term investment performance won't take long: just check out your super fund's annual report (which usually accompanies your super fund's member statement) for starters, or check out your super fund's website for the fund's latest investment returns and past investment performance.

Once you know this key bit of information, it can help you when you're planning how to reach your retirement savings target (see chapters 4 and 8). Knowing the long-term investment return of your super fund can help you work out how fast your superannuation savings will grow until you choose to retire (see step 5 of my Six-Step Wealth Check) and help you decide how big your final retirement balance needs to be to achieve your dream retirement (see step 3 of my Six-Step Wealth Check).

If your super fund's long-term performance is lower than you hoped for, or the risks associated with your super account's investment option are higher than you're comfortable with, then you can usually opt to change your super account's investment option (see tip 9).

Tip 9: Review your investment option, and change investment options, if necessary

If you don't take an interest in how your super fund invests your super savings, then your super fund will automatically invest your super money into a default investment option. If you have left the choice of investment option for your super account to your super fund, then you're in good company, because around 80 per cent of Australians don't exercise investment choice.

Who really invests your super money?

You may be surprised to hear that your super fund may not make specific investment decisions on your behalf. Often super funds work with asset consultants to decide on the asset mix of a super fund's different investment options, and then outsource the specific investment decisions within each investment option to fund managers. You can check out your super fund's website, or your super fund's annual report, to find out who is looking after your retirement savings.

The most common default investment options available in superannuation funds are the balanced or growth option. Typically, the balanced option invests 70 per cent of your money in growth assets, such as shares, listed property, and a small portion in alternative investments such as infrastructure. The remaining 30 per cent is usually invested in more conservative options such as cash and fixed interest. A typical growth investment option has around 80 per cent invested in growth assets and around 20 per cent in cash and fixed interest. Note that the terms growth and balanced are often used interchangeably by super funds.

The super fund returns that are regularly reported in the media are usually for the default balanced or growth options of major super funds. The general rule of thumb is that these investment options are suitable for most individuals who have more than seven years or so until retirement, and who can accept that returns may occasionally be in the negative.

If you're close to retirement, or you don't cope very well when your super account delivers a negative return (investment loss), then you may want to review your investment option, and shift your super savings to a more conservative investment option. Making such a decision is definitely dependent on each individual's unique circumstances. If you choose a more conservative investment option in your super fund, then over the longer term your final retirement benefit is likely to be smaller than a similar super account invested in a balanced or growth option.

If you're willing to take more risk to achieve a higher return over the longer term, then you may decide to actively choose a more aggressive investment option. In order of the most risky to the least risky, some of the typical investment options available in many large super funds include:

- aggressive

- high growth

- growth

- balanced

- conservative

- capital guaranteed.

Many super funds also give you the option of investing in specific asset classes, such as Australian shares, international shares or cash (visit SuperGuide at <www.superguide.com.au> for more information).

Warning

Different super funds may use different names for an investment option that carries the same level of risk, and invests in a similar asset mix. Always check with the super fund about what percentage of assets are in higher risk assets, such as shares and listed property, and what percentage are held in more conservative investments, such as cash and fixed interest, and whether that asset allocation reflects your understanding of the investment option.

Tip 10: Identify your dependants and non-dependants

Have you decided who will receive your super benefits if you die while a member of your super fund? You can nominate beneficiaries (recipients of your super benefits) now by completing special forms that you lodge with your super fund.

Although most people don't want to think about death, ensuring you have clear plans about what will happen to your super benefits after your death can potentially boost super payments to your surviving family members by thousands of dollars, and minimise the chance of disagreements between family members or complaints to your super fund over who receives your super benefits.

Doing some planning now can save your family a lot of stress and possibly save thousands of dollars in tax. Planning becomes especially important if you plan to leave your super benefits to someone that the tax laws do not class as a dependant, such as an adult child. If your super death benefits are paid to a dependant (under the tax laws), no benefits tax is payable. If your death benefits are paid to a non-dependant, tax is likely to be payable.

This is a very technical area of superannuation but it's worth doing some further reading if you intend to leave your super to independent adult children, or other non-dependants under the tax laws. Your super fund's website is a useful starting point for background information in this area.

Here are some basic facts to get you started:

- Your spouse (including your same-sex partner) is considered a dependant under the superannuation and tax laws, which means he or she can receive your super benefits tax-free upon your death. You can also receive your spouse's super benefits tax-free if they die.

- Your other dependants under the super and tax rules, such as your children under the age of 18 and financially dependent adult children, can also receive your super benefits tax-free if you die.

- Your non-dependants under the tax rules, such as independent adult children and other independent relatives, such as parents or siblings, are likely to pay up to 15 per cent tax on any death benefits they receive from your super fund. They will also pay up to 30 per cent tax on the portion of any superannuation death benefit payment that includes a life insurance payout. Up to 30 per cent tax will have to be paid when the death benefit is paid to a non-dependant from certain public sector super funds (see chapter 11).

- An adult child, or any other individual (such as a parent or sibling), can be deemed to be a dependant under the tax rules if they can prove they were financially dependent on the deceased fund member or they had an interdependent relationship with the deceased. An interdependent relationship is a close personal relationship between two people who live together, and where one or both provide for the financial and domestic support, and care of the other (visit SuperGuide at <www.superguide.com.au> for more information).

Strategies to rev up your super balance in a major way

By taking clear action, you can transform your financial future—potentially boosting your retirement savings by hundreds of thousands of dollars. The five tips below are some of the most popular superannuation strategies:

- *Tip 11:* Consider making concessional (before-tax) super contributions.

- *Tip 12:* Consider making non-concessional (after-tax) super contributions.

- *Tip 13:* Check if you're eligible for a co-contribution—a tax-free super boost from the government.

- *Tip 14:* Consider talking to an independent financial adviser, or an accountant.

- *Tip 15:* Consider setting up a self managed super fund.

Tip 11: Consider making concessional (before-tax) super contributions

The level of income you earn will generally determine whether you make before-tax (concessional) contributions or after-tax (non-concessional) contributions, or perhaps choose to make both types of super contributions.

From a tax savings point of view, concessional contributions are attractive if you pay more than 15 cents in the dollar tax on your income. In Australia, if you earn more than $37 000 (for 2011–12, or from 2012–13, earn more than $18 200, or $20 542 when you take into account the low income tax offset, subject to the legislation being passed), then your top rate of income tax is more than 15 cents in the dollar. If you earn more than $37 000 a year (for 2011–12), you can expect to pay at least 30 cents tax for each dollar earned above $37 000 (from 2012–13, you can expect to pay at least 19 cents in income tax for each dollar earned above $20 542, and 32.5 cents for each dollar earned above $37 000, subject to the legislation being passed; see the appendix for income tax rates).

Concessional contributions may also be a tax-effective option if you sell an investment and wants to offset a capital gains tax bill by putting all or part of the proceeds, subject to the contributions cap, into your super fund as concessional contributions.

You can make voluntary concessional contributions in one of two ways: by salary sacrifice, arranged through your employer, or tax-deductible contributions if you're self-employed.

If you're an employee, salary sacrifice is possible

Salary sacrificing is a popular strategy for employees earning middle to high incomes who want to increase their superannuation balances while reducing the amount of income tax they pay on their salary or wages.

Salary sacrifice is a voluntary arrangement between an employee and employer, and an employer does not have to consent to allowing you to salary sacrifice. Under a salary sacrifice arrangement, your employer makes additional contributions on your behalf when you arrange for some of your pre-tax salary to be paid into your super fund. Your salary for tax purposes is then reduced, while the additional contributions are treated as employer contributions. As employer contributions, you don't pay income tax on these amounts (although contributions tax of up to 15 per cent is deducted from the contribution when it goes into your super account) and your employer receives a tax deduction.

Splitting contributions with your spouse

An individual can make concessional (before-tax) contributions to a super fund and arrange to split those contributions with a spouse. If an individual plans to split super contributions with a spouse, then the receiving spouse must be under the age of 65. The person splitting the contributions must complete a form stating they intend to split their super contributions.

You can only split contributions made in the previous year. For example, contributions made during the 2011–12 year can only be split during 2012–13 (visit SuperGuide at <www.superguide.com.au>).

Warning

Some employees have to watch out that they don't lose their compulsory employer contributions (SG) in the process. A relatively unknown loophole in the SG rules enables an employer to cut an individual's SG entitlements when the employee reduces their taxable salary by salary sacrificing. In effect, by salary sacrificing, the cash component of a person's salary is reduced and the employer may choose to calculate the SG entitlement against the reduced cash component of the salary. The employee's total salary package is then smaller, unless the employee has a written contract specifying a total superannuation amount, or the employee works under an industrial award or collective agreement that states SG must be paid on the salary before the salary sacrificed contributions are deducted.

If you're self-employed or not employed, tax-deductible contributions are possible

Tax-deductible super contributions, like other concessional (before-tax) contributions, are subject to 15 per cent contributions tax within a super fund, which means that claiming a tax deduction for super contributions may not be tax effective if you pay less than 15 cents in the dollar tax on your income (see the appendix for income tax rates).

If you plan to claim a tax deduction for a super contribution, you must notify your super fund in writing before you lodge your tax return for the financial year, or by the end of the financial year following the year the contribution was made, whichever is earlier.

> ## Self-employed can split super with spouse too
>
> If you claim a tax deduction for super contributions you can also take advantage of the rules that permit a spouse to split her (or his) concessional super contributions with her (his) partner.

Watch the contributions cap

If you're considering making concessional contributions, you need to be mindful that these contributions are subject to an annual cap. If your concessional contributions exceed the concessional contributions cap, you will be hit with penalty tax (see table 10.1).

If you're an employee, your salary sacrificed contributions and your employer's SG contributions and any additional employer contributions count towards your concessional (before-tax) contributions cap. If you're self-employed (or not employed), then your tax-deductible super contributions for the year (July to June) are subject to the concessional cap.

Table 10.1: concessional (before-tax) contributions cap*

Income year	Cap for under fifties $	Cap for over fifties† $
2012–13	At least 25 000‡	At least 50 000, if account balance under 500 000
2011–12	25 000	50 000

*If you're aged 65 or over, you must satisfy a work test to make super contributions. You cannot make super contributions beyond the age of 74.

†Transitional provisions are in place (until 30 June 2012) for anyone aged 50 or over on or after 1 July 2007. The existing law states that from 1 July 2012, the contributions cap for all age groups is $25 000, plus any $5000 increments to the $25 000 limit due to indexation since 1 July 2009. The government has announced that the $50 000 (indexed) limit will remain in place for Australians aged 50 or over who have less than $500 000 in their super account (the legislation has not yet been passed).

‡For confirmation of the concessional contributions cap for the 2012–13 year and later years, please visit SuperGuide at <www.superguide.com.au>.

If you're under the age of 50, you can make concessional contributions worth up to $25 000 (for 2011–12) (indexed), before your contributions are hit with penalty tax of 31.5 per cent (in addition to the 15 per cent contributions tax). If you're aged 50 or over then you can make up to $50 000 in concessional contributions for 2011–12, before your contributions are hit with penalty tax (see table 10.1 on p. 167). From July 2012, the concessional cap for over fifties drops to $25 000, unless you have less than $500 000 in your super account (the legislation for the new over-fifties cap has not yet been passed).

Double trouble on caps

If you do exceed your concessional cap (see table 10.1), the excess concessional contributions also count towards your non-concessional (after-tax) contributions cap.

Tip 12: Consider making non-concessional (after-tax) super contributions

When you make a contribution to super from after-tax dollars, you're making a non-concessional contribution. The annual non-concessional contributions cap is $150 000 (for 2011–12), although it is possible to boost your non-concessional contributions for a particular year by taking advantage of the bring-forward rules. You can do this, for example, by making a $450 000 contribution in a single year, representing your entitlement for the next three years (see table 10.2), though that means you will not be able to make any contributions for the next two financial years without breaching the cap. Alternatively, you can trigger the bring-forward rules by making a $200 000 non-concessional contribution, or any contribution greater than $150 000 (for 2011–12). The bring-forward option is only available for those aged less than 65.

Small business owners can contribute more

If you're a small business owner you may also be eligible for a $1.205 million after-tax contribution limit for 2011–12 if you sell business assets, in addition to the non-concessional contributions cap. This amount is indexed so the limit increases each year, and it is a lifetime contribution limit. This permits personal contributions resulting from the disposal of small business assets. If you believe that you may be eligible then you will need to seek independent advice, most likely from an accountant, because the rules that apply to this exemption are complicated.

Co-contributions can be part of the package deal

If you make non-concessional contributions and your income is under a certain income threshold, you will receive a bonus co-contribution from the government (see tip 13).

Spouse contributions can save tax

If you or your spouse earns assessable income of less than $13 800, then your spouse or you can make super contributions on behalf of the low-income spouse and then claim a tax offset (offsets are amounts the ATO deducts from your tax bill, whereas a tax deduction is an amount the ATO allows to be deducted from your income). The maximum tax offset available is $540, when a spouse contributes $3000 or more to their low-income spouse's super account. If an individual receives $10 800 or less in assessable income, then his or her spouse can access the maximum tax offset of $540, provided an after-tax (non-concessional) contribution of at least $3000 is made. The tax offset is progressively reduced until the tax offset reaches zero for spouses who earn $13 800 or more in assessable income in a year (visit SuperGuide at <www.superguide.com.au).

Table 10.2: non-concessional (after-tax) contributions cap*

Income year	Cap $	Bring-forward rule $
2012–13	At least 150 000†	At least 450 000†
2011–12	150 000	450 000

* If you're aged 65 or over, you must satisfy a work test to make super contributions. You cannot make super contributions beyond the age of 74. You cannot take advantage of the bring-forward rule beyond the age of 65.

† For confirmation of the non-concessional contributions cap for the 2012–13 year and later years, please visit SuperGuide at <www.superguide.com.au>.

Tip 13: Check if you're eligible for a co-contribution — a tax-free super boost from the government

One of the best deals in super is the federal government's tax-free giveaway through its co-contribution scheme — the government will add a tax-free contribution to your super account if you make a non-concessional (after-tax) contribution, and you earn less than a certain level of income — for the 2011–12 year that was $61 920 (visit SuperGuide at <www.superguide.com. au> for income thresholds for 2012–13 and later years).

The government will pay up to $1000 when you make $1000 in non-concessional contributions in a financial year (12 months from July to June). You receive the maximum co-contribution if you earn less than the lower income threshold — for 2011–12 the lower income threshold is $31 920. The government pays $1.00 for every dollar you contribute to your super fund in after-tax dollars, up to a maximum of $1000 a year.

For example, if you make a $1000 non-concessional contribution and your income is below the $31 920 lower threshold, your super fund account will receive a $1000 tax-free contribution after you have lodged your tax return for that financial year. If you make a $600 contribution, the government will pay $600 into your super account. That's a 100 per cent return on your money! And you don't have to apply for the co-contribution, but you do have to lodge your income tax return before the government will pay the cash.

If you earn more than the lower income threshold, your co-contribution entitlement reduces by 5 cents for every dollar you earn over this threshold, until it eventually cuts out entirely. For the 2011–12 year, the co-contribution cuts out at an income of $61 920.

Tip 14: Consider talking to an independent financial adviser, or an accountant

You don't have to get advice when choosing super funds, or when considering making extra super contributions, or for any other financial matters.

If you do want financial advice, however, then do some research on what to look for in an adviser, and talk to friends about reputable advisers. Advisers deserve to be paid for providing advice, but a planner who receives commissions on the products they sell to you, rather than a fixed fee for providing advice, is representing a super fund or other financial company as well as advising you. In short, use an adviser that charges a fee rather than collects commissions.

If you're making major financial decisions, particularly decisions that could have significant tax implications inside or outside super, then consider seeking independent tax advice from an accountant or superannuation advice from a financial adviser who understands the super rules and charges a fee for advice rather than accepts commissions from product providers for giving you advice. Independent advisers are difficult to find, but not impossible (visit SuperGuide at <www.superguide.com.au>).

Use a tax agent for tax advice

If you're seeking tax advice, and many superannuation strategies involve tax advice, then an accountant who is a registered tax agent is a more appropriate expert than a financial adviser.

Tip 15: Consider setting up a self managed super fund

Running a self managed superannuation fund (SMSF) gives you control over where your super money is invested, as well as access to a wider choice of direct investments compared with investing through managed super funds, such as retail or industry funds. As an SMSF trustee, you can invest in direct property, artworks and virtually any valuable asset. You can even purchase business property, such as an office, and use the property in your business (if you have one).

Before you get too excited about the positives of running an SMSF, you need to ask yourself three key questions:

1 Will you be able to commit the time and energy to running the fund over the long term?

2 Are you familiar with investing?

3 Do you have lots of money, that is, superannuation money — at least $250 000?

These questions may sound pretty heavy, but running an SMSF is a serious commitment. After all, you may be running your fund for more than 50 years — longer than most marriages — if you're going to pay yourself a pension, or income stream, from your SMSF in retirement.

Choosing to run your own fund usually means that you're confident you can deliver better returns than the professionals. As trustee of your SMSF you must draft an investment strategy, follow special investment rules and choose, and record, investments that will deliver you a retirement benefit when you finish work.

If you run your own self managed super fund (SMSF) when you retire, you will have to manage your own retirement savings including running a pension and making pension payments. For some women, having total control over retirement savings may be an exciting prospect. For other women, worrying about the super rules and managing paperwork associated with running an SMSF is not what they had in mind for the dream retirement.

Two types of DIY super fund

The term DIY super fund is a nickname for what is officially known as a self managed superannuation fund (SMSF). Assuming you have the right to choose your own super fund, setting up an SMSF is one of your super options. You can also choose another type of DIY super fund, known as a small APRA fund, although that's a less popular option. A professional trustee runs a small APRA fund, and the Australian Prudential Regulation Authority regulates the professional trustee and fund. A small APRA super fund costs more to run than an SMSF, because you have to pay trustee fees, although the trustee fee usually includes any administration and compliance costs. Keep in mind that DIY super is not for beginner investors. If you know nothing about investing, a DIY super fund is not the place to begin your investment lessons.

As a handy reference, I have included a one-page checklist of the 15 tips covered in this chapter. If a checklist of 15 tips looks daunting, remember that the list has been designed so you can approach your super-boosting plan in three stages:

- super quick fixes that can save you thousands of dollars (tips 1 to 5)

- simple, and free, super strategies that can help you build a larger nest egg (tips 6 to 10)

- strategies to rev up your super balance in a major way (tips 11 to 15).

Super checklist — 15 tips to help you create a cushy retirement

- [ ] Give your tax file number (TFN) to your super fund, so you won't pay unnecessary tax.

- [ ] Find out how many super funds you have, and update your contact details.

- [ ] Consider combining your super accounts to reduce how much you pay in fees.

- [ ] Check that your employer is making compulsory super contributions (SG) for you, and that the amount is correct.

- [ ] Check your life insurance cover in your super fund.

- [ ] Do a financial stocktake for today and for tomorrow — work out how much money is enough, and whether your existing super strategies will leave you with a financial gap between what you will have and what you want.

- [ ] Review your fund — is your super fund good enough for your retirement plans? If not, consider changing your super funds.

- [ ] Check your super fund's investment returns.

- [ ] Review your investment option, and change investment options, if necessary.

- [ ] Identify your dependants and non-dependants.

- [ ] Consider making concessional (before-tax) super contributions.

- [ ] Consider making non-concessional (after-tax) super contributions.

- [ ] Check if you're eligible for a co-contribution — a tax-free super boost from the government.

- [ ] Consider talking to an independent financial adviser, or an accountant.

- [ ] Consider setting up a self managed super fund.

Chapter 11

What happens when I retire? Super benefits, the Age Pension, tax and other stuff

> 66 She who laughs last at the boss's jokes probably isn't far 99 from retirement.

Anonymous

'When I retire' is a phrase that often precedes happy thoughts about what we plan to do when we finish working, or when we finish raising children, or when we finish doing both. In chapter 1, I shared my own retirement dream and listed a bunch of fantastic retirement plans that women have shared with me over the years. Here are a few more examples of dreams that women have shared with me that start with the phrase 'When I retire':

- I'm going to live beside the coast and walk barefoot in the sand every day.

- I want to spend more time with my children and grandchildren.

- I would love to spend six months of each year in Europe.

- I want to play more golf. I want to play more tennis [or insert your sport of choice].

- My aim is to climb Mount Everest.

- I want to have a vacation that's not scheduled to suit the school holidays.

- I want to be able to help communities in impoverished countries.

- I'm going to live in a Native American tepee.

- I am going to sleep for a week.

- I am going to stay up all night if I want.

- I am going to read every book in my bookcase, and then buy
  more books.

The retirement plans we may daydream about remind me in many ways of the dreams that children have when they imagine what they will do 'when I grow up'. I don't mean that the retirement dreams are childish — not at all! What I mean is that the closer you get to adulthood, the more realistic your dreams generally become for when you grow up. Likewise, the dreams you may have for retirement will become a lot more specific, and possibly more practical, the closer you get to the time that you do plan to retire.

Dreams can still come true, but you're now at the business end of making your dreams become reality. One of the basic practicalities is what happens to you financially when you retire — in particular, how long will your retirement money last?

Remember, retirement is *not* the last step before the grave. You can expect to spend nearly as many years in retirement as you probably did in the workforce, or in raising children, or doing both.

This chapter provides a snapshot of some of the financial issues you need to think about before retiring, including:

- Are you planning to retire early?

- How long does your money have to last?

- When can you access the Age Pension?

- When can you access your superannuation benefits?

- What tax (if any) do you pay on your super benefits when you retire?

- What tax (if any) do you pay on your non-superannuation income
  and savings?

> ## Tip
>
> You may be eligible for other financial benefits in retirement, including healthcare discounts, pensioner concessions on gas, electricity and water bills, discounted travel and discounts on retail purchases. You can visit the government website for over fifties at <www.seniors.gov.au> for more information on the types of discounts available.

Are you planning to retire early?

The big difference between working and retirement is that you're not receiving a regular pay cheque (and your partner is not receiving a pay cheque) in retirement. Depending on the age that you retire, you can expect your income in retirement to come from one or more of the following sources (in no particular order):

- part-time work, if you choose
- income from a superannuation pension
- regular Age Pension payments
- income from an overseas pension scheme
- income from savings and investments
- generous relatives or friends.

You can retire at any age you wish, but if you retire before you can access your super benefits, or before you can access the Age Pension (if you're eligible), then you will need to rely on your private savings to survive. Do you have enough savings to last until you can claim your super benefits or the Age Pension? Do you have enough money to give you the standard of living that you seek for this longer life in retirement?

In Australia, retiring early can have the following financial implications:

- no access to the Age Pension until you reach Age Pension age (ranging from age 64 to 67)
- no access to superannuation benefits until you reach your preservation age (ranging from age 55 to 60)

- higher taxes on superannuation benefits if you retire before the age of 60, rather than if you wait until age 60 to retire

- potentially higher taxes on non-superannuation savings for the years in retirement before you reach Age Pension age.

How long does your money have to last?

Clearly, an important decision when planning for retirement is deciding on the age at which you intend to retire, and then working out how long you will live in retirement. The earlier you retire, the more money you will need to finance a longer retirement.

A popular rule of thumb when planning how much money you need to have to finance your retirement is to plan for your money to last at least until you reach your average life expectancy — that is, how long you can expect to live, on average (see table 11.1).

Consider the following scenarios:

- If you retire at 65, then you can expect to live another 22 years (until age 87, give or take a few months), on average.

- If you retire at 67, then you can expect to live another 20 years (until age 87), on average.

- If you retire at 55, then you can plan for another 30.5 years (until age 85.5) on this planet.

Tip

About half of all women currently aged 65 or 67 will live longer than 87 years, while the other half will die before they reach the age of 87. That may sound a bit depressing, but the upside to the life expectancy statistics is that the longer you live, the better your life expectancy becomes. For example, a woman aged 75 has an average life expectancy of 13.5 years, which means since she was 65, she has increased her life expectancy (statistically) by 18 months to 88.5 years, simply by getting on with life.

Here is another example. A 70-year-old female can expect to live two years longer than a woman who is currently 55 years of age. Such a statistic does not mean that we are dying younger — not at all! The younger you are, the shorter your life expectancy due to the law of averages. An average life expectancy is simply an average for the population, and the older you get the more chance there is that that you're in the healthier half of the population, which generally means that your chances are greater (than the average person's) for living beyond the average life expectancy for each age group.

If you're aged 55, your average life expectancy is 30.53 years, that is, you're expected to live to 85.53 years. If you reach the life expectancy age that was estimated when you were 55, then you have outlived about half of those Australians who were also aged 55 years, 30 years earlier. At 85 years, your average life expectancy is now 91 years. A female planning to retire at the age of 55 could potentially live for at least another 36 years — more years than many women spend in the workforce.

Table 11.1: average life expectancies

Females			Males		
Current age	Years to live	Life expectancy age	Current age	Years to live	Life expectancy age
55	30.53	85.53	55	26.95	81.95
57	28.70	85.70	57	25.20	82.20
60	26.00	86.00	60	22.63	82.63
65	21.62	86.62	65	18.54	83.54
67	19.92	86.92	67	16.99	83.99
70	17.42	87.42	70	14.76	84.76
75	13.51	88.51	75	11.31	86.31
80	10.01	90.01	80	8.38	88.38
85	7.08	92.08	85	6.03	91.03
87	6.11	93.11	87	5.27	92.27
90	4.91	94.91	90	4.36	94.36

Source: Average life expectancies extracted from Australian Life Tables, 2005–2007, Australian Government Actuary (released in November 2009 and updated every five years; the next update is in 2014). The table structure and life expectancy ages were compiled by the author. Visit <www.superguide.com.au> and type 'life expectancy' into the search function for the complete list of life expectancies, from birth through to age 109.

How long you live, or you're expected to live, is often called your longevity. In the super world, the money men use the term longevity risk to describe the possibility of outlasting your retirement savings. For you, longevity risk can be a good thing because it means that you're living longer, although it has financial consequences when you don't have enough savings to support you for that amount of time.

When can you get the Age Pension?

If the Age Pension is a big part of your financial plans in retirement, then the timing of your retirement becomes very significant. You can access the Age Pension only when you reach your Age Pension age, assuming that you're eligible.

You must actively apply for the Age Pension, and to be eligible for this regular Age Pension payment, your income and any assets that you own (excluding the home you live in and other property), must be below set financial thresholds.

What is your Age Pension age?

For women, the Age Pension age has been progressively increased from the age of 60 (up to the mid 1990s), and it will eventually reach the age of 67 by 2023 (see table 11.2).

Table 11.2: what is your Age Pension age?

Age Pension age	Affecting women born	Age Pension age commencement date
60 to 63.5	Before January 1946 (see Centrelink for more details)	
64	From 1 January 1946 to 30 June 1947	1 January 2010
64.5	From 1 July 1947 to 31 December 1948	1 January 2012
65	From 1 January 1949 to 30 June 1952	1 January 2014
65.5	From 1 July 1952 to 31 December 1953	1 July 2017
66	From 1 January 1954 to 30 June 1955	1 July 2019
66.5	From 1 July 1955 to 31 December 1956	1 July 2021
67	From 1 January 1957 onwards	1 July 2023

Source: Table created from information published on the Centrelink website at <www.centrelink.gov.au>.

The essential points in table 11.2 are as follows:

- If you were born on or after 1 January 1949 and before July 1952, then your Age Pension age is 65 years.

- If you were born on or after 1 January 1957, then your Age Pension age is 67.

- If you were born any time between January 1946 and December 1948, then your Age Pension age is 64 or 64.5 years.

- If you were born after June 1952 but before January 1957, then your Age Pension is one of three options — 65.5, 66, or 66.5 years.

Can you satisfy both of the Age Pension wealth tests?

Reaching your Age Pension age is not the only hurdle to jump if you're planning to claim the Age Pension when you retire. You must also satisfy an income test and an assets test, which are administered by Centrelink. Individuals and couples are subject to different financial thresholds.

Age Pension assets test

Although the prospect of a test may sound intimidating, around 80 per cent of all retired Australians receive a full or part Age Pension. At the time of writing, a single person who owns their own home can have around **$670 000** in assets (in addition to her home) and still claim a part Age Pension. A couple can have nearly **$1 million** in assets (plus the home they live in and own) and claim a small part Age Pension. Under the assets test, your car, household contents and other lifestyle assets are counted when assessing your Age Pension entitlements.

Age Pension income test

At the time of writing, a single person can earn around **$41 000** a year in income and still be able to claim a small part Age Pension. A couple can earn a combined income of more than **$62 000** a year and still be able to claim a small part Age Pension.

If your income is above the income test threshold, or you own assets worth more than the assets test threshold, you may still be eligible for the Age Pension in the later years of your retirement (Visit SuperGuide at <www.superguide. com.au> for more information).

Tip

An eligible individual must satisfy both the Age Pension income test, and the Age Pension assets test to receive a full, or part, Age Pension. The amount of Age Pension you get is based on the test that delivers the lower amount on Age Pension entitlement. If you fail one of the tests, then you will not be eligible for the Age Pension. Couples are subject to the same tests, although higher income and asset thresholds apply to them than to singles. In June 2011, a full Age Pension was worth around **$18 960** a year for a single person, and around **$28 590** a year for a couple.

Clean energy supplement for retirees

In July 2011, the federal government announced the introduction of a carbon tax on Australia's biggest polluting companies. The government said that more than half the revenue raised from the carbon tax will be redirected to Australians in the form of tax cuts and a clean energy supplement. The tax cuts (see the appendix for tax rates) and supplement are designed to compensate Australians for the expected cost increases that will be passed onto consumers when the carbon tax is introduced from July 2012.

Assuming the laws are passed, from July 2012, Australians eligible for the Age Pension will be paid a clean energy supplement of up to $338 for singles and $510 for couples (combined), split into fortnightly payments. Retirees who do not receive the Age Pension but who hold a Commonwealth Seniors Health Card will also receive the clean energy supplement.

When can you access your super benefits?

You can access your superannuation benefits as a lump sum or as a superannuation pension, or take part of your super benefit as a lump sum, and part as a pension. A pension is a series of regular payments over time (but it is different from the publicly funded Age Pension). A pension paid from a superannuation benefit is sometimes called an income stream.

The special rules that apply to superannuation mean that you cannot access your super benefits as a lump sum or pension until you reach a certain age (your preservation age) and retire, or satisfy another condition of release. A condition of release is an event that allows you to withdraw your benefits.

Age pension: are you planning to rent in retirement?

If you plan to rent a house or flat or other type of accommodation during your retirement, then thinking about what happens when you retire becomes even more important. You may need to take into account this additional expense when calculating how much money you will need, including where you plan to live.

One of the upsides of renting is that you don't have to worry about ongoing costs, such as council rates and house maintenance, but you do lose control over where you can live. Landlords can evict you if they want to move into their property, or if they want to renovate the property, or if they want to sell the property. You may also be hit with rental increases that you're not comfortable with, or can't afford.

If you do rent a home in retirement, you're permitted to own more assets than a home-owner under the Age Pension assets test when claiming the Age Pension. This increase in the assets test threshold for renters recognises that rent can take a big chunk out of your retirement income.

A single person who is renting can own around $800 000 in assets before losing all Age Pension entitlements. In contrast, a single home-owner must have around $670 000 in assets before they will lose Age Pension entitlements. A couple who rent can own more than $1.1 million in assets and still receive a part Age Pension, while a home-owning couple lose Age Pension entitlements if their assets exceed around $1 million.

A recipient of the Age Pension may also be eligible for rent assistance. According to Centrelink, rent can include private rent, site fees, boating fees, maintenance fees in a retirement village, and board and lodging rates. Generally, you cannot receive rent assistance if you're already living in public housing. Contact Centrelink or visit <www.centrelink.gov.au> for more information about renting in retirement.

Wait for your preservation age

If you're planning to retire and you want to withdraw your super benefits, then you must have reached your preservation age to access your super benefits.

Your preservation age is based on the year that you were born. For anyone born before 1 July 1960, the preservation age is 55. The preservation age steadily increases until it reaches 60 years of age for those born on or after 1 July 1964 (see table 11.3, overleaf).

Table 11.3: what is the minimum age for accessing super benefits?

Date of birth	Your preservation age
Before 1 July 1960	55
From 1 July 1960 until 30 June 1961	56
From 1 July 1961 until 30 June 1962	57
From 1 July 1962 until 30 June 1963	58
From 1 July 1963 until 30 June 1964	59
On or after 1 July 1964	60

Source: Created from information available on the Australian Taxation Office superannuation website <www.ato.gov.au/super>.

Tip

You don't have to withdraw your superannuation benefits by a certain age. You can choose to leave your super account untouched indefinitely. If this is what you decide, your super account will remain in what's called an accumulation phase. Accumulation phase means that you haven't started a pension from your superannuation account. If you make this decision, however, your super account's earnings will continue to be subject to up to 15 per cent tax on fund earnings, because the fund assets remain in accumulation phase. In contrast, earnings on super benefits in pension phase are free of tax on earnings later in the chapter.

Satisfy a condition of release

Although you must have reached your preservation age to access your super benefits, merely reaching that specified age is not enough to unlock your super benefits. Your super benefits remain preserved until you satisfy a condition of release. Preserved for the purposes of superannuation simply means locked away, rather than protected or guaranteed.

Satisfying a condition of release means your preserved benefits can become unrestricted or unlocked—that means you can access your super, provided the rules of your fund also let you cash your super. The most common conditions of release are:

• *Deciding to retire on or after preservation age.* You have unlimited access to your super benefits when you retire on or after your preservation age. Depending on your birth date, preservation age can be age 55, 56, 57, 58, 59 or age 60. Retirement generally involves signing a retirement declaration that you have ceased a full-time employment arrangement and that you never intend to be gainfully employed for more than 10 hours per week. You must send the declaration to your super fund.

- *Ceasing employment on or after the age of 60.* Special retirement rules apply for an individual who terminates an employment arrangement after the age of 60. Where a person is aged 60 or over, but less than 65, and she ceases an employment arrangement, then she can be considered to have retired for the purposes of accessing preserved super benefits. If an employment arrangement continues, however, then turning 60 on its own is not considered a condition of release.

- *Reaching the age of 65.* By turning 65 you can have unlimited access to your super benefits as a lump sum or pension, and you don't have to retire if you don't want to.

- *Starting a transition-to-retirement pension (which I call a TRIP).* TRIPs are special superannuation pensions that allow individuals aged 55 to 64 to continue working while drawing down their super benefits as a pension. The maximum amount that can be withdrawn each year is 10 per cent of your account balance, and a minimum amount must be withdrawn each year. If you later choose to retire then you can have unlimited access to your super benefits, including being able to take out lump sums from your super. Taking a TRIP can have tax advantages for some women, but you should chat to your accountant or super fund about this option.

Tip

Although most super benefits are preserved until you reach preservation age *and* satisfy a condition of release, some Australians who had superannuation accounts before 1999 may also have some benefits known as non-preserved benefits. If you have non-preserved benefits, then the benefits will either be restricted non-preserved (which you can access when you terminate your employment), or unrestricted non-preserved benefits (which you can access at any time). You can check with your super fund if you believe your super benefits may include some non-preserved benefits.

If an individual is suffering severe financial hardship, or at risk of losing their home, there are limited circumstances available to access super benefits to help the individual cope financially.

Warning

Nitty gritty tax section ahead! If you're not interested in reading about tax and retirement, then you may want to consider skipping the rest of this chapter and heading to chapter 12. If you're within 10 years of retirement, however, the next few pages explaining a potentially tax-free life in retirement are valuable reading. Make yourself a cuppa, take a deep breath and read on. Alternatively, take a break and read it tomorrow.

What tax do you pay on your super benefits when you retire?

To make the most of the tax benefits in super, the key age you need to be mindful of when retiring is age 60 — and what matters is whether you retire *on or after* the age of 60, or whether you retire *before* the age of 60. Generally speaking, super benefits are tax-free when paid *on or after* the age of 60, while super benefits are subject to tax when paid *before* the age of 60, unless you receive super benefits from one of the older public sector super funds.

Tip

Although it may be tempting to withdraw all of your superannuation when you retire and even go on a spending spree, it could end up costing you tens of thousands of dollars in lost future earnings and lost tax benefits. A key advantage of keeping your money in the super system when you retire is that you enjoy double tax-free benefits. What I mean by this is that you have two sources of tax-free superannuation benefits. The earnings on super fund assets are exempt from tax when you start a super pension. In comparison, if you invest your savings outside the super environment, the earnings on your savings are potentially subject to income tax, up to your marginal tax rate. The second is that your income in retirement is tax-free when it comes from your super benefits. In short, you receive tax-free income, and your tax-free income is sourced from assets that are invested in a tax-free environment.

Retiring *on or after* the age of 60

If you're aged at least 60 and you retire, you can receive your superannuation benefits tax-free — as a lump sum or as a pension — assuming your super benefits are from a taxed source. Most Australians are members of a taxed super fund (the exception is if you have been a member of one of the older public sector funds — see the box below).

Not only can you take your super benefits free of tax after the age of 60, those superannuation benefits don't count towards your income for the purposes of paying income tax on your non-superannuation income. Confused? What this means is that your super benefits after age 60 are not included in your annual tax return. You may also be able to take advantage of the tax-free income threshold for income tax, and the low income tax offset (LITO). As a result, you can expect to pay little or no tax on income you may earn in retirement from sources other than super, depending on your level of income. For example, you can receive $60 000 income as pension payments from your super fund, plus **$16 000** (for the 2011–12 year, or **$20 542** from 2012–13, subject to the legislation being passed) in non-super income from part-time work or investments and pay no tax due to the combination of:

- tax-free super

- the tax-free income threshold of **$6000** (for 2011–12, or **$18 200** from 2012–13 year, subject to the legislation being passed)

- low income tax offset (LITO).

If you have reached Age Pension age, you can earn a lot more non-super income and still pay no tax thanks to the senior Australians tax offset (SATO).

Warning

If your super benefits are paid from an untaxed source (such as some of the older public sector funds looking after older employees including teachers, emergency services and health workers, and other public servants) then your benefits may still be subject to benefits tax and income tax after you turn 60 (see the box on p. 192).

Retiring *before* the age of 60

If you retire before the age of 60, your super benefits are likely to be subject to some tax, depending on the components of your super benefit.

Your super benefit can potentially be made up of two components — a tax-free component and a taxable component. The tax-free component is always tax-free and it generally is made up of after-tax super contributions you have made to the fund (including one-off after-tax contributions that you may make from an inheritance or other financial windfall). The taxable component is potentially taxable and it is made up of your employer's compulsory super contributions (SG), plus any concessional (before-tax) super contributions that you make, plus the fund's earnings on your total super account.

How much tax you can expect to pay on your superannuation benefit when you withdraw your super before the age of 60 depends on whether:

- you take your super benefit as a lump sum or a super pension

- your super benefit includes a tax-free component

- you're a member of one of the older public sector super funds.

> # Warning
>
> The next paragraph is fairly technical so you may need to reread it a couple of times, or scan it, and come back later. Or, if you're not interested in retiring before the age of 60, pretend you didn't see it and head directly to the next section.

If you choose to retire before you turn 60, then you can expect the following tax implications:

- *Taking a lump sum.* If you take your super as a lump sum, the first $165000 (for 2011–12) of your taxable component is tax-free, except for certain benefits paid from older public sector super funds. The tax-free limit of $165000 is known as the low-rate cap, and it is indexed each year. The low-rate cap is a lifetime limit, which means that once you have used up the tax-free limit, tax is payable on the taxable component of lump sums taken before the age of 60.

- *Receiving a benefit that includes a tax-free component.* The tax-free component is always tax-free. The tax-free component represents your non-concessional (after-tax) contributions and, if you were a member of a fund before July 2007, the tax-free component may also include several other elements of your pre-July 2007 super benefit.

- *Taking a super pension (income stream).* If you're under the age of 60, payments from a superannuation pension are taxed differently from a super benefit that you take as a lump sum. If you retire before the age of 60, payments from your pension count towards your taxable income, subject to two tax concessions. The tax-free component (if any) of your super benefit will not be subject to income tax. The taxable component of your pension will be eligible for a 15 per cent pension offset. The pension offset reduces your income tax bill — possibly even to zero.

- *Receiving a benefit from an untaxed source means a bigger tax bill.* Most Australians receive super benefits from a taxed source, but about 10 per cent of all super accounts are from an untaxed source (mainly older public sector super funds). The taxable component of super benefits paid from an untaxed source is subject to higher rates of tax (see the box on p. 192).

You can find more information on the tax implications of taking super benefits before the age of 60 and receiving super benefits from an untaxed source by visiting the ATO website <www.ato.gov.au/super> or by visiting my website, SuperGuide at <www.superguide.com.au>.

What tax do you pay on your non-super income and savings?

Even when you retire, the taxman may still want his share of your income. The good news is that the taxman is likely to take a much smaller cut (if any) after you reach a certain age.

If you retire before the age of 60

If you're under the age of 60 when you retire, you can expect to be treated like any other taxpayer. Like everyone else, you pay no tax on the first $6000 of your income (for 2011–12, or $18 200 from 2012–13 year, subject to the legislation being passed), and then the rest of your income is taxed at different rates up to your top marginal tax rate. For 2011–12 your top marginal tax rate can be 0 per cent, 15 per cent, 30 per cent, 37 per cent or 45 per cent (from 2012–13, your top marginal tax rate can be 0 per cent, 19 per cent, 32.5 per cent, 37 per cent or 45 per cent, subject to the legislation being passed). Your super benefits will also count towards your assessable income for income tax purposes, although you can expect some super tax concessions.

If you retire before reaching Age Pension age

If you're under Age Pension age when you retire, you can expect to be treated like any other taxpayer, with one major exception. Like other taxpayers, you can earn non-super income of up to $16 000 (for 2011–12, or up to $20 542 from 2012–13) before any income tax is payable, and you will be subject to income tax up to your marginal tax rate on higher levels of income.

If you're aged 60 or over, however, your superannuation pension or lump sum from a taxed source is not included as part of your assessable income, which means you can have a much higher tax-free income in retirement by receiving your super benefits tax-free, and then also taking advantage of the tax-free income tax threshold of $6000 (for 2011–12, or $18 200 from 2012–13), and the low income tax offset.

> ## Tip
>
> The low income tax offset (LITO) is available to all eligible taxpayers. The effective tax bill is nil for those earning up to $16 000 (for the 2011–12 year), because they will be eligible for the maximum LITO ($1500 for 2011–12). The LITO gradually reduces as assessable income increases, and LITO is no longer available when assessable income reaches $67 500 (for 2011–12; see the appendix for the LITO for later years).

If you retire on or after reaching Age Pension age

The tax rules are more generous when you reach your Age Pension age. If you're Age Pension age, you may be able to access a more generous tax-free threshold called the senior Australians tax offset (SATO). The SATO reduces the tax payable on income for eligible taxpayers. This means that any individual who has reached Age Pension age needs to work out whether they're eligible for the SATO. An individual who has reached Age Pension age (65 for men, and from January 2012, 64.5 years for women) may be eligible for the SATO.

If a person is eligible for the SATO, then they can expect to receive a tax offset (a reduction in the tax payable) for all or part of their total income tax provided their income falls within the SATO income threshold. Some individuals can expect to pay no tax at all, or pay a lower amount of tax, compared with someone who is not eligible for SATO. For the 2011–12 year, the SATO can mean:

- Singles can earn just over **$30 000** in non-superannuation income without paying any income tax because of the application of SATO and LITO. Remember, this tax-free income is in addition to your tax-free super benefits. Not bad!

- Couples can earn just under **$27 000** each (nearly **$54 000** combined) per year without paying income tax on non-super income, and subject to certain conditions.

- A couple earning income higher than **$54 000** a year or so may still be eligible for the SATO, but they will receive a lower tax offset, which means that some tax is generally payable. SATO applies to income of up to around **$48 000** for a single person and around **$79 000** (roughly

$39 500 each) for a couple, which means at these levels of income you still pay tax, but not as much as you would without the benefit of the offset.

Warning

If your non-super income exceeds the SATO thresholds, then your non-super income is subject to the same marginal tax rates as the rest of the population (see appendix and SuperGuide).

More tax for retired public servants

If you're a long-term teacher, nurse or public servant, or an employee of the defence forces, or you work for the emergency services or in other public service jobs, then you may need to check whether you're a member of an untaxed fund. The government estimates that around 10 per cent of Australian workers are members of one of the older public sector untaxed superannuation schemes.

If you're a member of an untaxed super fund, then it is likely you will have to pay some tax on super benefits when you retire, even when you receive your super benefits on or after the age of 60. Although paying tax is a bit of a downer (I explain why tax is payable at the end of this section), this type of super fund also usually offers guaranteed income streams for life in retirement, known as a defined benefit pension, and then another lifetime pension (known as a reversionary pension) to your partner after you die. The potential to receive a guaranteed lifetime pension from a super fund is a rare and valuable benefit.

You can expect the following tax treatment when receiving benefits from an untaxed super fund:

- *Retiring on or after age 60.* If you take a lump sum, the taxable component of your benefit is taxed at 15 per cent up to the untaxed plan cap of $1 205 000, and then the top marginal tax rate (45 per cent) for benefits above the $1.205 million cap (for 2011–12). If you take a pension using an untaxed benefit, the taxable component of your pension income is taxed at marginal tax rates, although you're entitled to a 10 per cent pension offset. The tax-free component of your benefit is returned to you over time as tax-free amounts.

- *Retiring before age 60.* If you take a lump sum, you may pay 15 per cent or 30 per cent tax, or both, on the taxable component depending on the size of the benefit and the age that you retire. If you receive more than $1.205 million (for 2011–12), your benefit above this amount is taxed up to the top marginal tax rate of 45 per cent. If you start a pension using an untaxed benefit before the age of 60, then you're not eligible for the 10 per cent pension offset, until you turn 60.

The reason that certain super funds are known as untaxed funds is because the government hasn't yet paid in the cash for the additional employer contributions it has agreed to pay on behalf of employees. Instead, a notional amount is recorded as a member's entitlement for the additional employer contributions that the government has contracted to contribute to the untaxed super funds. Upon retirement, this part of the member's benefit, and notional earnings based on a special benefit formula, is paid out of consolidated revenue (more commonly known as money collected from taxpayers to run the Australian government). Benefits from an untaxed source are then subject to higher rates of tax to recoup the contributions and earnings taxes that were not collected during the working life of the fund member. These older untaxed schemes are now closed to new members.

Chapter 12

Next step—financial freedom!

> *What this day says to Australian women and Australian girls is that you can do anything, you can be anything, and it makes my heart sing to see women in so many diverse roles across our country in Australia.*

Quentin Bryce, on becoming Australia's first female Governor-General

Not boring at all! At least that's what one of my test readers had to say about this book.

Before finalising *Super Freedom*, I asked seven female friends to test the book against their own circumstances, which included the needs of single, married, divorced and gay women. My generous friends also tested the book against the challenges facing women raising children, women with little or no super, women working part time or not at all, and women on low or above-average incomes. The feedback from these women was invaluable, and their general and specific comments assisted me in fine-tuning the case studies and clarifying the key messages contained throughout the book.

Here's an example of some general feedback from one of my test readers: 'The book was easy to read and very positive. It was very informative in a simple way, and I learnt a lot from it. Good to know that there is still hope if you're older and have a low super balance. It wasn't boring at all, as I thought it was going to be—no offence!'

No offence taken: I consider the feedback a compliment considering that my friend enjoyed reading the book, and would not normally have bothered with picking up a super book. Before reading *Super Freedom*, this friend believed that superannuation wouldn't cater for her circumstances. You may recall that, in chapter 1, I wrote that many women initially find the concept of superannuation boring, until they discover what super can deliver in terms of financial freedom.

I trust that, like my test readers, you found *Super Freedom* helpful and not as boring as you thought it might have been. In fact, I'm expecting that the book has motivated you to start thinking seriously about your financial security, and has inspired you to take the next steps in achieving financial freedom in retirement.

Don't stop just yet. If you haven't already done so, why not:

- try my Six-Step Wealth Check at home
- seek out further information on superannuation and investing
- seek financial advice if you need it.

Try the Six-Step Wealth Check at home

Now is the perfect time to apply my Six-Step Wealth Check to your own circumstances. Your six-step process doesn't have to be perfect on your first attempt, but have a go and see how far you can get — you may be pleasantly surprised by what you discover.

Even when you have a gap between your retirement expectations and what your current circumstances will deliver, you can dramatically improve your financial future by doing a little or a lot, or perhaps by doing heaps. In the appendix, I explain how to use each of the free ASIC MoneySmart calculators, which were used for the calculations throughout this book.

Seek out further information

You can use *Super Freedom* as a hands-on reference when doing your own superannuation planning. The further you investigate your financial needs, the greater your level of knowledge will become, and the more questions you can expect to have.

SuperGuide — free website on superannuation

If you're looking for further information on superannuation and how you can make the super rules work for you, then my free super website, SuperGuide <www.superguide.com.au>, can answer many of the questions Australian women have about superannuation. You can also subscribe to the *SuperGuide* monthly email newsletter. It's free!

LearnerInvestor—free website on investing, for beginners

If you're interested in learning more about how your super fund invests your super money then your first step is to visit your super fund's website.

Alternatively, if you want to know more about investing generally, including how super funds invest the $1 trillion-plus Australians already have in super savings, then you may be interested in my free consumer website, LearnerInvestor at <www.learnerinvestor.com.au>, designed for those new to investing, or new to an aspect of investing. You can subscribe to the free *LearnerInvestor* email newsletter.

Other useful websites

In Australia, we are fortunate that both sides of politics believe in the importance of financial education for consumers. The following federal government websites can also help you with your retirement planning:

- *MoneySmart* <www.moneysmart.gov.au>. ASIC's MoneySmart website is designed to help 'ordinary Australians take steps to improve their personal finances' and provide information so 'you can be better informed in making decisions', according to the 'About us' section on the MoneySmart website. The website also operates the free online calculators that I refer to throughout the book.

- *Australian Tax Office* <www.ato.gov.au/super>. The ATO runs the key government website for consumer information on superannuation and tax (visit the 'Individuals' section). The ATO website is also the key government site for those individuals choosing to run a self managed super fund (visit the 'Super funds' section).

- *Centrelink* <www.centrelink.gov.au>. You can find information about the Age Pension, including all the details on the income and assets tests, as well as the latest payment rates. Centrelink also operates an excellent free information service, including free seminars, covering retirement planning and investing, called the Financial Information Service.

- *NICRI* <www.nicri.gov.au>. NICRI stands for the National Information Centre on Retirement Investments. It provides free information on planning and saving for retirement, and also information on investing during retirement.

Seek financial advice if you need it

At some stage in your retirement planning, you're likely to want to, or need to, talk to a specialist. You have several options if you need expert advice about your wealth accumulation or retirement plans, including the following individuals or organisations:

- *Your accountant.* If you use an accountant for your tax affairs, then he or she can be a useful sounding board for any tax management strategies involving super, such as salary sacrifice arrangements and the tax implications when you retire and take super benefits. Accountants often help clients run self managed super funds.

- *Your super fund.* Your super fund may provide a separate financial planning service offering full investment and retirement advice to fund members. Check whether your super fund can provide advice on all aspects of retirement planning, or whether the licence is restricted to services related to your super fund only. Your super fund may also offer a more limited intra-fund advice service. Intra-fund advice involves authorised staff in your super fund, providing advice on fund-specific decisions, such as insurance cover, nomination of beneficiaries for the purposes of death benefits, and pension advice.

- *Licensed and fee-based financial adviser.* Always choose a licensed financial adviser, and check that the financial adviser charges you a fee for the advice rather than takes a cut from your super savings in the form of commissions. Although currently rare in the Australian financial adviser community, an independent adviser can offer you financial advice free of conflicts of interest. Check my SuperGuide website at <www.superguide.com.au> for more information on how to spot an independent adviser.

I hope this book helps you to help yourself in creating a better life in retirement—a worry-free financial future. I wish you all the best.

Appendix:
A short guide to the free calculators, table assumptions and tax rates

Read on to discover how to use the free online calculators that I refer to throughout the book, to uncover the assumptions behind nearly every table appearing in this book, and to check out the latest income tax rates, including the latest round of tax cuts taking effect from July 2012.

A short guide to the free calculators

Throughout *Super Freedom*, I use the ASIC MoneySmart calculators to illustrate how doing nothing (only having compulsory employer super contributions, that is, superannuation guarantee), doing a little, or doing a lot (and even doing heaps) can deliver a worry-free financial future.

I very much enjoyed creating the case studies because the calculators enabled me to convert the super theory into practical examples, demonstrating how easy it can be to transform your financial circumstances in retirement through regular superannuation contributions.

In this book, I used three ASIC MoneySmart calculators:

* superannuation calculator

* retirement planner calculator

* account-based pension calculator.

The calculators are free to use and available on the MoneySmart website at <www.moneysmart.gov.au>. When using each calculator, I applied certain assumptions and sometimes these assumptions varied depending on the case study or the topic I was explaining. For example, I generally used the age of 67 or 65 when assuming retirement age.

In this appendix, I explain how you can use the three calculators listed above to conduct your own Six-Step Wealth Check, including default assumptions that you need to be mindful of when applying your own financial circumstances. Later in this appendix, I list the customised assumptions that I used in each table and each case study throughout the book.

Some other MoneySmart calculators, which I have not used in this book, include:

- compound interest calculator

- super vs mortgage calculator

- super co-contributions calculator.

Tip

ASIC provides another free online calculator, the MoneySmart compound interest calculator, which I have not used in this book, but it may be useful for estimating how your existing non-super savings have grown. Compound interest is when you earn interest on your reinvested interest income. By reinvesting interest or investment earnings (to create compound earnings), you can accumulate wealth faster because your savings base continues to grow. The MoneySmart compound interest calculator can estimate what your non-super savings will be worth at a future date if you reinvest all the interest you earn. The calculator can estimate a future value for a one-off amount, or for an investment where you make regular additional investments. The one flaw with the compound interest calculator is that it doesn't take fees and taxes into account, although it is possible to fiddle with the calculator to allow for after-tax returns.

Tip

You can change nearly all of the assumptions in the calculators if you wish. You can assume a higher investment return, if you are willing to take greater risks, or change the level of fees that you pay, or the level of insurance premiums (if any) that you pay. You can also change the annual inflation rate and how much you earn, or how much you want to receive as income in retirement.

> ## Tip
>
> In all of the tables, I have assumed 3 per cent inflation. The incomes, contributions and lump amounts have been adjusted to allow for 3 per cent cost of living increases each year, to reflect today's dollars—what your savings would be worth when comparing what you can buy with that money today. The default assumption in all calculators is 3.5 per cent (2.5 per cent inflation and 1 per cent increase in living standards above inflation).

ASIC MoneySmart superannuation calculator

You can use the ASIC MoneySmart superannuation calculator (see figure A1, overleaf) to work out how much superannuation you can expect to have when you retire, or reach a certain age. Your superannuation balance will be presented as a lump sum amount.

The superannuation calculator can tell you:

- what your employer's contributions plus earnings (less fees and taxes) will deliver you by the time you retire

- what impact making your own super contributions can have on your final retirement balance.

> ## Tip
>
> Employer contributions (SG obligation) are set at the equivalent of 9 per cent of a person's salary. The federal government plans from July 2013, however, for the SG to increase to 9.25 per cent, and then gradually increase to 12 per cent by July 2019 (though the legislation has not yet been passed). For the example used in figure A1 (overleaf), 9 per cent works out at $4500 a year in employer contributions.

Figure A1: the ASIC MoneySmart superannuation calculator

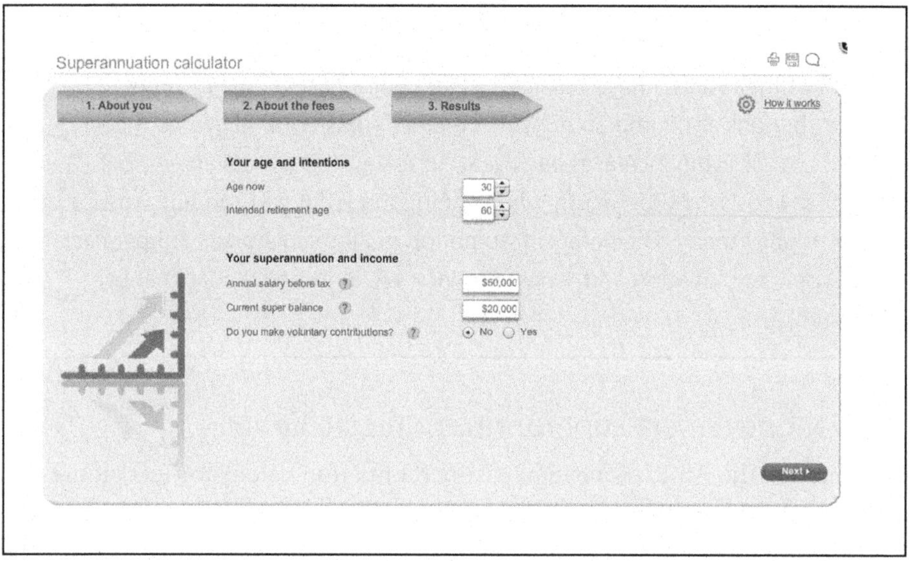

Source: MoneySmart website <http://www.moneysmart.gov.au>, 30 June 2011. Reproduced with permission of ASIC.

You need the following information to use the superannuation calculator:

- your age

- your intended retirement age

- annual salary before tax

- current super balance

- amount of super contributions that you make (if any), and whether you make those contributions as a percentage of your salary, or as a dollar amount each week, fortnight, month or year.

Default assumptions for MoneySmart superannuation calculator

The superannuation calculator uses the following default assumptions:

- Management fees are 0.5 per cent of the account balance each year, and a $50 a year administration or management fee is also charged.

- Employer contributions are 9 per cent of the gross (before-tax) annual salary. The calculator automatically deducts the 15 per cent contributions tax from employer contributions.

- Insurance premiums of $100 are deducted each year.

- Super savings are invested in a balanced investment option, which delivers 7.5 per cent before tax. The calculator assumes 9 per cent earnings tax is deducted from investment returns.

- Inflation rate is 2.5 per cent and rise in living standards is 1.0 per cent, which means lump sum amounts are presented in today's dollars.

- Before-tax or after-tax voluntary super contributions can be included in the calculation.

- Calculator cannot be used for defined benefit super funds. Most Australians are not members of defined benefit funds.

My customised assumptions

Throughout this book, I have modified the default assumptions for the superannuation calculator as follows: investment returns are 7 per cent after fees and taxes, which means the fees and earnings tax boxes are set at zero, and the investment return is set at moderate. No insurance premiums are deducted, and inflation and cost-of-living adjustments are set at 3 per cent rather than 3.5 per cent.

ASIC MoneySmart retirement planner calculator

You can use the ASIC MoneySmart retirement planner calculator (see figure A2, overleaf) to work out what your lump sum (final retirement balance) can deliver you in the form of an annual income in retirement. The annual income includes a full or part Age Pension (if eligible, and most Australians will be eligible).

Clean energy supplement increases Age Pension

From July 2012 a person's Age Pension entitlement will include a clean energy supplement (subject to the legislation being passed). This means that the annual Age Pension amounts and annual retirement incomes that include an Age Pension entitlement quoted throughout the book will increase by up to $338 in today's dollars for a single person, and around $510 in today's dollars for a couple. That is in addition to the regular six-monthly adjustment to the Age Pension rates.

Figure A2: the ASIC MoneySmart retirement planner calculator

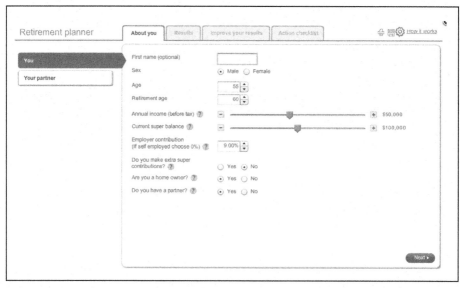

Source: MoneySmart website <http://www.moneysmart.gov.au>, 30 June 2011. Reproduced with permission of ASIC.

Tip

You can change all of the variables, such as your life expectancy, your desired income, your retirement age, whether you expect to have a partner, and whether you want to take into account the Age Pension.

Tip

The MoneySmart retirement planner calculator assumes that in retirement money is retained in the superannuation system and paid out as a retirement income stream (superannuation pension). Under the super rules, investment earnings in pension phase are tax-free, and pension payments from retirement income streams received after the age of 60 are free of income tax.

The retirement planner calculator can tell you:

- your expected annual income in retirement
- how much Age Pension you can expect to receive

- the combination of Age Pension and superannuation to deliver you the maximum income

- how long your money will last at a set level of income.

You need the following information to use the retirement planner calculator to work out your expected annual retirement income:

- lump sum amount on retirement (using the superannuation calculator). In this book, I use the superannuation calculator to work out the final lump sum, and then the retirement planner to work out annual retirement income. Using my approach, you insert your lump sum amount as the current super balance and then adjust the 'About you' section by setting your age as the same age as your retirement age and set the annual income (before tax) at zero dollars

- current super balance. You can also use the retirement planner to calculate your accumulated super savings and what those super savings will deliver to you as an annual retirement income, but the retirement planner does not disclose the final lump sum you accumulate on retirement. If you choose to use the retirement planner in this way, then you will need the information listed as necessary under the superannuation calculator. Throughout the book, I use the superannuation calculator for this purpose

- retirement age

- whether you are a home-owner on retirement

- whether you have a partner (affects how much Age Pension that you receive)

- your life expectancy, or how long you want your money to last

- how much you want to spend in the first year (if any) before you start an income stream.

Default assumptions for MoneySmart retirement planner calculator

The retirement planner uses the following default assumptions:

- that management fees are 0.5 per cent of the retirement account balance each year, and a $50 a year administration/management fee is also charged

- that retirement savings are invested via a conservative investment option delivering 6.5 per cent return

- you are a home-owner

- retirement income includes the Age Pension. In this book, case studies apply Age Pension rates (including pension supplement) for singles and couples as at 20 March 2011. Age Pension rates are adjusted twice yearly, in March and September. Assume individual or couple own personal assets of $25 000, in addition to your home. Note that Age Pension age rises to age 67 from 2023

- you have a partner

- your money runs out at age 90

- inflation rate is 2.5 per cent and rise in living standards is 1.0 per cent which means annual incomes are presented in today's dollars

- you spend a few thousand in the first year before you start your income stream. Note that I can't work out this assumption and there doesn't seem to be any pattern to the amount chosen to be spent by the calculator. I always set this amount at zero. You need to click a few 'Next' buttons to have this box pop up, and you can make your own decision about how much you plan to spend (if any) in your first year of retirement before you start your pension.

My customised assumptions

Throughout this book, I have modified the default assumptions for the retirement planner calculator as follows. Investment returns are 7 per cent after fees and taxes (that is, reinvested) on the account balance of a superannuation pension, which means the fees boxes are set at zero, and the investment return is set at moderate. Inflation and cost of living adjustments are set at 3 per cent rather than 3.5 per cent. Money lasts until age 87, or age 100, or whatever age I use in the relevant case study. No money is spent in year one before commencing the retirement income stream.

ASIC MoneySmart account-based pension calculator

You can use the ASIC MoneySmart account-based pension calculator to work out what your superannuation savings can deliver you in the form of an annual income in retirement. (An account-based pension is the most popular type of superannuation pension. It requires you withdraw a minimum amount each year.) You may want to use this calculator rather than the retirement planner calculator if you are not expecting to receive the Age Pension, and plan to rely solely on your superannuation pension.

The account-based pension calculator is a handy tool to work out what your super savings can deliver if you are planning to retire early, or you expect to have substantial super savings (precluding Age Pension eligibility). Retaining your savings in the superannuation system means you can expect to receive your retirement income free of tax (except for some public servants). Curiously, the account-based pension calculator uses slightly different default assumptions from the retirement planner in terms of investment return and fees. See the default assumptions, overleaf.

The account-based pension calculator can tell you:

- your expected annual income in retirement

- how long your money will last at a set level of income

- what level of income you can expect if you want your money to last until a specified age

- the minimum payment required to be withdrawn from your super pension each year.

- when your annual income will fall by 5 per cent below target income, when your account-based pension falls below $10 000 a year, and when it drops to zero.

Tip

The account-based pension calculator can be more difficult to use than the other MoneySmart calculators because it is run via an Excel program. This added complexity, however, means that you have more flexibility in adjusting the assumptions and also greater access to the workings behind the annual calculations, which may help you understand further how the retirement rules work.

You need the following information to use the account-based pension calculator to work out your expected annual retirement income:

- age you plan to start your account-based pension

- final super account balance, that is, how much money you are planning to use to start the pension

- income that you want to receive.

Default assumptions for MoneySmart account-based pension calculator

The account-based pension calculator uses the following default assumptions:

- Management fees are 0.55 per cent of the retirement account balance each year, and a $55 a year administration or management fee is also charged.

- Retirement savings are invested in a balanced investment option delivering 8.0 per cent return before fees.

- Inflation rate is 2.5 per cent and rise in living standards is 1.0 per cent, which means annual incomes are presented in today's dollars.

- In retirement, money is retained in the superannuation system and paid out as a retirement income stream. Under the super rules, investment earnings in pension phase are tax-free, and pension payments from retirement income streams received after the age of 60 years are free of income tax.

My customised assumptions

Throughout this book, I have modified the default assumptions for the account-based pension calculator as follows. Investment returns are 7 per cent after fees and taxes (that is, reinvested) on account balance of account-based income stream, which means the fees boxes are set at zero, and the investment return is set at moderate. Inflation and cost of living adjustments are set at 3 per cent rather than 3.5 per cent. Money lasts until age 87, or age 100, or whatever age I use in the relevant case study. No money is spent in year 1 before commencing the retirement income stream.

A short guide to the assumptions used in tables and text

For ease of reference, I have set out the assumptions used in the text and in tables in the order of appearance in the book. You can look for the chapter and then the relevant sub-heading or table heading.

More Age Pension from July 2012

From July 2012, a person's Age Pension entitlement will increase to include a clean energy supplement (subject to the legislation being passed). This means that the annual Age Pension amounts, and annual retirement incomes that include an Age Pension entitlement quoted in the tables and text throughout the book will increase by up to $338 in today's dollars for a single person, and around $510 in today's dollars for a couple. That is in addition to the regular six-monthly adjustment to the Age Pension rates.

Chapter 2 Getting the monkeys off your back: what's stopping you from taking super control?

The amounts quoted in Monkey 3 were calculated using:

- ASIC MoneySmart superannuation calculator (for lump sum amounts). My customised assumptions were used and all other assumptions used were default assumptions, except in the last example, where employer contributions are used, the individual earns $50 000 a year and works and receives compulsory employer super contributions for 30 years.

- ASIC MoneySmart retirement planner calculator (for annual retirement income, including Age Pension entitlements). My customised assumptions were used and all other assumptions used were default assumptions, except that retirement income from super savings lasts from the age of 65 until the age of 87 (female life expectancy at age 65 and at age 67), or until the age of 100, and then the individual relies solely on Age Pension.

Chapter 3 Investing for super beginners

The assumptions used in table 3.2 are:

- The amounts for future years are in future dollars: the figures are not in today's dollars, apart from the final amounts for year 10, which are in future dollars, and today's dollars. Today's dollars are what your future money would be worth if you spent it today. The year 10 figures have been rounded to the nearest $500.

- The figures for example 4 were calculated using the ASIC MoneySmart superannuation calculator. My customised assumptions were used and all other assumptions used were default assumptions, except Renee is age 45, and super contributions are $5895 less 15 per cent contributions tax, which means $5011 is paid into Renee's account each year, in quarterly instalments.

- For simplicity, and to be conservative in calculations, example 4 assumes Renee receives 9 per cent SG for the 10-year period, although she can expect the SG to increase by 0.25 per cent from July 2013 (to 9.25 per cent) and then by 0.5 per cent increments each year until it reaches 12 per cent from July 2019 (subject to legislation). If Renee received 12 per cent SG for the 10-year period her final balance would be **$193841**, which in today's dollars amounts to **$154502**. In reality, Renee's super balance will be somewhere between **$170000** and **$194000** because she won't receive 12 per cent SG for the full 10-year period.

Chapter 4 Your Six-Step Wealth Check: how much money is enough?

The assumptions used in table 4.2 are:

- Your Age Pension age is 65 or 67. The Age Pension age (the age at which you can claim the Age Pension) is increasing over time. Anyone born after December 1948 and before July 1952 has an Age Pension age of 65, while anyone born on or after 1 January 1957 has an Age Pension age of 67 years. Anyone born between these dates has an Age Pension age of 65.5, 66, or 66.5 years. If you were born before January 1949, then your Age Pension age is 64.5 years or less (see chapter 11 for more details).

- You retire at the age of 65 (assuming that your Age Pension age is 65), or 67 (if 67 is your Age Pension age) and that your superannuation money runs out 22 years later. If you retire at age 65, then the lump sum amounts in table 4.2 should last until you reach the age of 87 (22 years later)—a female's average life expectancy at age 65. If you retire at the age of 67, then the lump sum in the table should last until the age of 89 (22 years later).

- If you live beyond the age of 87 (or 89, if Age Pension age is 67), then table 4.2 assumes you rely solely on the Age Pension. In chapter 11, I explain how knowing your life expectancy (how long you may live on average) can help you plan for retirement.

- The lump sum amounts are in today's dollars.

- If eligible for Age Pension (see Receives Age Pension column), your target retirement amount depends on how much Age Pension you receive each year, and the level of investment earnings when you invest your target retirement amount, on retirement. See below for further assumptions used in table 4.2.

- Income tax is not reflected in table 4.2, because the amounts assume annual income is taken as an income stream (pension) from a superannuation fund, which is tax-free on or after the age of 60. In many cases, tax is not relevant for retirees even when they receive non-super income.

Target income and retirement amounts listed in table 4.2 are compiled from sources as follows:

- Age Pension rates (including pension supplement) for singles and couples as at 20 March 2011. Age Pension rates adjusted twice yearly, in March and September. Assume individual or couple own personal assets of $25 000.

- Modest and comfortable target annual incomes (as at September 2010) are based on the ASFA Retirement Standard (at <www.superannuation.asn.au>). The annual income figures (latest figures available as at May 2011), are adjusted periodically in line with the cost of living.

- Target retirement amounts needed when No Age Pension were calculated using ASIC's MoneySmart account-based pension calculator. My customised assumptions were used and all other assumptions used were default assumptions except the account-based income stream runs out at the age of 87 (life expectancy for a 65-year-old female). If your Age Pension age is 67, then assume the money runs out after 22 years, at 89 years. If you live beyond 87 (or 89), then you will rely only on the Age Pension. Calculations for No Age Pension do not take into account any tax payable or Age Pension.

- The target retirement amounts when Receives Age Pension in table 4.2 were calculated using ASIC's MoneySmart retirement planner calculator for the lower lump sum amounts of the comfortable lifestyle figures for a single person and for a couple. The figures from the No Age Pension column are used as upper lump sum amounts in the comfortable category if Receives Age Pension. Again, my customised assumptions were used and all other assumptions used were default assumptions except the income stream from a super fund runs out at the age of 87 when you retire at 65, or runs out at age 89 when you retire at the age of 67. If you live beyond 87 (or 89), then you will rely on only the Age Pension. For couple figures, assume both members of the couple are age 65 (or age 67 if eligible for Age Pension at age 67).

The lump sums necessary to finance the annual retirement incomes quoted in Good News Alert no. 4 (see p. 49) were calculated with the ASIC MoneySmart retirement planner. My customised assumptions were used and all other assumptions used were default assumptions, except that the retirement income lasts until the age of 87. After reaching 87, the individual relies solely on the Age Pension.

Chapter 5 Case study—I'm 52. Is it too late to start saving?

The table 5.1 lump sum calculations are made using the ASIC MoneySmart retirement planner calculator. The assumptions used in table 5.1 are:

- Irene's Age Pension age is 67, and Irene retires at the age of 67.

- Age Pension rate (including pension supplement) for singles as at 20 March 2011. Age Pension rates are adjusted twice yearly, in March and September. Assume Irene owns personal assets of $25 000.

- Modest and comfortable target annual incomes (as at September 2010) are based on the ASFA Retirement Standard (ASFA website at <www. superannuation.asn.au>). The annual income figures (latest figures available as at May 2011) are adjusted periodically in line with the cost of living.

- The lump sum amounts needed for income until age 87, and for income until 100, were calculated using ASIC's MoneySmart retirement planner and include a full Age Pension for a modest lifestyle, and a substantial part Age Pension for all other target annual incomes. My customised assumptions were used and all other assumptions used were default assumptions, except the income stream from a super fund runs out at the age of 87, or runs out at age 100, and Irene relies only on the Age Pension.

Tables 5.2, 5.3 and 5.4

This section discusses the assumptions for these three tables:

- Table 5.2: Irene banks on 15 more years of super guarantee payments

- Table 5.3: Irene contributes an extra $100 a week to her super fund and creates a familiar lifestyle in one easy step

- Table 5.4: Irene contributes an extra $100 a week for five years, then $200 a week for 10 years to create a comfortable lifestyle.

The assumptions used in tables 5.2, 5.3 and 5.4 are:

- Super account balances were calculated using the ASIC MoneySmart superannuation calculator. My customised assumptions were used and all other assumptions used were default assumptions.

- In tables 5.3 and 5.4, non-concessional (after-tax) contributions are made monthly ($433 or $866 a month) but are the equivalent of weekly contributions of $100 or $200 a week).

- Annual retirement incomes were calculated using the ASIC MoneySmart retirement planner calculator. My customised assumptions were used and all other assumptions used were default assumptions except the income stream from a super fund runs out at the age of 87, or runs out at age 100, and after reaching 87, or 100, Irene relies only on the Age Pension.

- Irene's Age Pension age is 67, and Irene retires at the age of 67.

- The annual incomes in table 5.2 include a full Age Pension, and in tables 5.3 and 5.4, a substantial part Age Pension.

Chapter 7 Doing a little: turn $4500 into $300 000 the easy way

This section discusses the assumptions for the following tables:

- Table 7.1: Chrissy's super balance if she does nothing, a little, heaps or has a work break (age 25, nil starting balance, income $50 000 a year)

- Table 7.2: Julie's super balance if she does nothing, a little, a lot or heaps and retires at 60, or retires at 67 (age 35, $15 000 starting account balance, income $50 000 a year)

- Table 7.3: Sahn's super balance and retirement income based on doing nothing, a lot, or heaps, retiring at 67 (single), or retiring at 67 (as a couple) (age 45, $15 000 starting account balance, earns $50 000 a year)

- Table 7.4: Lily's super balance and retirement income if she does nothing, a lot, or heaps and retires at 65, or retires at 70 (age 55, $70 000 starting balance, income $50 000 a year).

The lump sum amounts and annual retirement amounts appearing in tables 7.1, 7.2, 7.3, and 7.4 were calculated using the following calculators.

- ASIC MoneySmart superannuation calculator (for lump sum amounts). My customised assumptions were used and all other assumptions used were default assumptions except that calculations assume after-tax (non-concessional) contributions are made in a single lump sum at the beginning of the financial year.

- ASIC MoneySmart retirement planner calculator (for annual retirement income, including Age Pension entitlements). My customised assumptions were used and all other assumptions were default assumptions except that annual retirement income amount listed in text and tables lasts until age 87, or age 100 (as indicated) and when this age (87 or 100) is reached, the individual relies only on the Age Pension.

Chapter 8 Doing a lot—Making $1 million is possible, but it takes a super plan

The assumptions used in table 8.1 are:

- Tax rates applied are the 2011–12 income tax rates. Visit the Australian Taxation Office website at <www.ato.gov.au> or SuperGuide at <www.superguide.com.au> for the income tax rates for later years. The income tax payable does not include any tax rebates available such as the low income tax offset, or family tax benefits.

- The lump sums necessary to finance the retirement target were calculated using the ASIC MoneySmart retirement planner calculator. My customised assumptions were used and all other assumptions used were default assumptions except that annual retirement income amount listed in the text and tables lasts until age 87, and when this age is reached, the individual relies only on the Age Pension.

Table 8.2: How much money is enough for a worry-free retirement, with no Age Pension?

The lump sum amounts in table 8.2 were calculated using the ASIC MoneySmart account-based pension calculator. My customised assumptions were used and all other assumptions used were default assumptions except:

- Lump sum amounts in the table assume no receipt of Age Pension, although at the lower income levels some Age Pension may be available on retirement, and the Age Pension is generally available at nearly all income levels in the later years of retirement.

- Annual retirement income amount listed in text and tables lasts until age 87, or until age 100, and when this age is reached, the individual relies only on the Age Pension.

Chapter 9 Case studies — four women create $1 million nest eggs

The lump sum amounts and annual retirement amounts appearing in the text and tables of this chapter were calculated using the following calculators:

- ASIC MoneySmart account-based pension calculator

- ASIC MoneySmart superannuation calculator (for lump sum amounts)

- ASIC MoneySmart retirement planner calculator (for annual retirement income, including Age Pension entitlements).

ASIC MoneySmart account-based pension calculator

When using ASIC's account-based pension calculator to compile tables 9.1, 9.3, 9.6 and 9.9, and to calculate retirement incomes sourced from lump sum amounts greater than $1 million in tables 9.2 and 9.4, my customised assumptions were used and all other assumptions used were default assumptions except that lump sum amounts in tables 9.1, 9.3, 9.6 and 9.9 assume no receipt of Age Pension, although at the lower income levels, some Age Pension may be available on retirement, and Age Pension is generally available at nearly all income levels in the later years of retirement (see chapters 8 and 9 for further explanation).

ASIC MoneySmart superannuation calculator

When using ASIC's superannuation calculator to compile the lump sum amounts for tables 9.2, 9.4, 9.5, 9.7, 9.8 and 9.10, my customised assumptions were used and all other assumptions used were default assumptions except:

- Compulsory employer contributions SG are set at the equivalent of 9 per cent of a person's salary for their working life. The government intends that from July 2013, the SG will increase to 9.25 per cent, then gradually increase to 12 per cent by July 2019 (the legislation has not yet been passed).

- Calculations assume before-tax (concessional) contributions are made monthly throughout the financial year.

- Calculations assume after-tax (non-concessional) contributions are made in a single lump sum at the beginning of the financial year.

ASIC MoneySmart retirement planner calculator

When using ASIC's MoneySmart retirement planner calculator to compile the annual retirement incomes for tables 9.2, 9.4, 9.5, 9.7, 9.8 and 9.10, my customised assumptions were used and all other assumptions used were default assumptions except:

- Annual retirement income figures under No Age Pension are subject to the same assumptions as Part Age Pension calculations, apart from the fact that the annual retirement income does not include a part Age Pension.

- Annual retirement income amount listed in text and tables lasts until age 87, or age 100 (as indicated) and when this age is reached (87 or 100), the individual relies only on the Age Pension.

Latest income tax rates

Table A1 (overleaf) lists the income tax rates for the 2011–12 financial year (1 July to 30 June), and the proposed tax rates for the 2012–13 financial year through to the 2015–16 financial year.

In July 2011 the federal government announced changes to the tax system as part of the government's plan for a clean energy future. If the legislation is passed, from July 2012 anyone earning less than $20 542 will not pay income tax, after taking into account the tax-free threshold and the low income tax offset (LITO).

Table A1: income tax rates

Tax scales	2011–12*		2012–13		2015–16	
	Threshold $	Marginal rate	Threshold $	Marginal rate	Threshold $	Marginal rate
1st rate	6001	15%	18201	19%	19401	19%
2nd rate	37001	30%	37001	32.5%	37001	33%
3rd rate	80001	37%	80001	37%	80001	37%
4th rate	180001	45%	180001	45%	180001	45%
LITO	Up to $1500	4% withdrawal rate on income over $30000	Up to $445	1.5% withdrawal rate on income over $37000	Up to $300	1% withdrawal rate on income over $37000
Effective tax-free threshold**	16000		20542		20979	

Source: Office of the Deputy Prime Minister and Treasurer 2011, Joint media release with Prime Minister (No. 081) 10 July 2011, 'Combining tax cuts with significant tax reform'.
*For the 2011–12 year only, if your taxable income is greater than $50 000, you will also be taxed with a flood levy of at least 0.5 per cent.
**Includes the effect of the tax-free threshold and the low income tax offset (LITO).

Glossary

account-based pension   The most popular type of superannuation pension. A series of regular payments from a superannuation fund account. The rules require that a minimum pension amount is paid each year.

accumulation phase   The period of time when a super account is growing in anticipation of the fund member's retirement at some later date. In short, a superannuation account that is not in the pension phase.

after-tax return   The investment return after any tax payable on that return has been deducted.

Age Pension   A guaranteed taxpayer-funded pension for eligible Australians, paid fortnightly by the government.

Age Pension age   The age at which you can apply for the Age Pension, determined by your date of birth.

aggressive investment option   A higher risk investment option that has a higher allocation to growth assets such as shares and property.

APRA   The Australian Prudential Regulation Authority, which is the main superannuation regulator.

ASFA   The Association of Superannuation Funds of Australia, which is the major superannuation industry association.

ASFA Retirement Standard (Retirement Standard)   Measures the cost of a modest or comfortable lifestyle in retirement, based on the lives of actual retirees.

ASIC   The Australian Securities and Investments Commission, which is a corporate, investment markets and financial services regulator.

asset allocation   How your super fund divvies up your super money into different asset classes for investment.

asset(s) and asset classes   The different categories of investments, such as cash, shares and property.

assets test for Age Pension   The value of your assets must be below a certain threshold for you to be eligible for a full or part Age Pension.

Australian Taxation Office   The ATO monitors employers to ensure they meet SG obligations, provides information on superannuation on its website for consumers, monitors breaches of contribution caps, and regulates self managed super funds.

balanced investment option   Most super fund members have their money in this type of option. Super money is invested in a mix of higher risk assets, such as shares and property, and lower risk assets, such as cash and fixed interest.

capital guaranteed investment option   A lower risk option that promises to preserve your initial super savings, generally at the cost of lower returns.

carbon tax   In July 2011 the federal government announced the introduction of a carbon tax on Australia's biggest polluting companies, to take effect from July 2012 (subject to the legislation being passed). As a means of offsetting the possible cost increases for consumers, the government is introducing substantial tax cuts from July 2012 and also introducing a clean energy supplement for Age Pensioners and other retirees.

Centrelink   Government agency that administers the Age Pension and other retirement-related allowances, and also runs the Financial Information Service.

clean energy supplement   From July 2012 a person's Age Pension entitlement will include a clean energy supplement (subject to the legislation being passed), to help offset the cost increases associated with the introduction of a carbon tax. This means that the annual Age Pension amounts will increase by up to $338 in today's dollars for a single person, and around $510 in today's dollars for a couple, in addition to the regular six-monthly adjustments to the Age Pension rates.

co-contribution scheme   When you make a non-concessional (after-tax) contribution to a super fund, and your annual income is below a certain threshold, the federal government will deposit tax-free money into your super account after you lodge your tax return.

comfortable lifestyle   Based on the ASFA Retirement Standard, a comfortable lifestyle can be achieved in retirement when you have an annual after-tax income of about $54 000 for a couple, and $39 000 for a single person.

Commonwealth Seniors Health Card (CSHC) The holder of a CSHC pays a concessional price for prescriptions under the Pharmaceutical Benefits Scheme and receives the clean energy supplement (subject to the legislation being passed). The card is available to Australians of Age Pension age who don't receive the Age Pension and earn less than the income threshold for the card.

company (or corporate) super fund A super fund run by a company for its employees; such a super fund is not available to the general public.

compound earnings or compound interest The earnings that you earn on top of your initial investment earnings or bank interest or other type of investment return. By reinvesting earnings or interest, you can accumulate wealth faster because your investment base continues to grow.

concessional (before-tax) contributions Any superannuation contribution where an individual or company receives a tax deduction for making the super payment.

condition of release Preserved super benefits cannot be withdrawn unless you satisfy a condition of release, such as retiring, turning 65, starting a transition-to-retirement pension, suffering severe financial hardship, to name a few.

conservative investment option A lower risk investment option with a higher allocation to cash and fixed interest and a lower allocation to shares and property and other higher risk assets.

contributions caps The super contributions that you can make are subject to caps. If you exceed those caps, the contributions above your cap are hit with excess contributions tax.

death benefits Superannuation benefits paid on the death of a super fund member. Benefits are generally paid to a spouse, or other dependants or non-dependants.

default fund The super fund where your employer's SG contributions are deposited if you do not choose your own fund.

default investment option The investment option where your money is placed for investment if you do not make an investment choice.

defined benefit   A superannuation benefit that is not dependent on investment returns but is determined by a formula based on years of service and salary.

dependant   A person eligible to receive death benefits when a fund member dies. If an individual is also a dependant under the tax laws, such as a spouse or financially dependent relative, then they can receive the death benefits free of tax.

diversification   Spreading the risk over several asset classes and across different investments.

doing nothing   For the purposes of this book, the term doing nothing relates to turning up for work and receiving SG contributions, but not making your own voluntary super contributions.

Financial Information Service   A free information service on retirement options and retirement planning administered by Centrelink.

future dollars   What you receive in the future without adjusting the amount for inflation.

growth assets   Higher risk investments, such as shares and property.

high growth investment option   An investment option available in the large super funds, with a higher allocation to growth assets such as shares and property.

income protection insurance   Insurance available in some super funds, and outside super funds, that pays you an income for a period of time, typically for up to two years, if you have an accident or are too sick to work.

income stream   *see* pension.

income tax-free threshold   The level of income that you can earn before you have to pay income tax.

income test for Age Pension   The income you receive must be below a certain threshold for you to be eligible for a full or part Age Pension.

industry super fund   A super fund that typically caters for workers from a particular industry, although many of them are now available to anyone.

inflation   Rising prices over time, usually measured by the Consumer Price Index (CPI).

interdependent relationship A close personal relationship between two people who live together, and where one or both provide for the financial and domestic support and care of the other.

investment choice The opportunity to place your super money in a variety of investment options offered by your super fund.

investment options The different types of pre-mixed investment portfolios offered by super funds.

investment portfolio A collection of investments a person or super fund may hold.

investment return The profit or interest or earnings from an investment.

life expectancy or **longevity** or **average life expectancy** How long you can expect to live on average based on statistical data from the office of the Australian Government Actuary.

life insurance Insurance available in and outside super funds that pays a lump sum or pension (in some cases) when a fund member dies. In a super fund, life insurance is often combined with permanent disability insurance. Large super funds can often offer these types of insurance at cheaper rates than you could negotiate as an individual outside super.

low income tax offset (LITO) An offset against tax payable for taxpayers who have taxable income below a certain threshold. The maximum LITO is $1500 (for 2011–12 year).

lump sum A one-off payment from a superannuation fund.

marginal tax rate The highest rate of income tax that you pay on your income, ranging from 0 per cent to 45 per cent, plus up to 1.5 per cent Medicare levy.

master trust An investment vehicle that gives you access to a lot of managed funds, rather than a single investment.

mature aged worker tax offset (MAWTO) An offset available for Australians age 55 or over who are still in the workforce.

maximum contributions base If you earn big bucks, then your SG entitlement is subject to a cap. For the 2011–12 year, an employer is required to make SG contributions on 9 per cent of salary up to an annual salary limit of $175 280 ($43 820 each quarter).

modest lifestyle   Based on the ASFA Retirement Standard, a modest lifestyle can be achieved in retirement when you have an annual after-tax income of about $31 000 for a couple, and $21 000 for a single person.

negative return   An odd term to describe when your super account suffers an investment loss (drop in value) rather than an investment gain (increase in value).

nominated beneficiary   Eligible person or persons you identify to be paid your super benefits if you die.

non-concessional (after-tax) contributions   Super contributions where you haven't claimed a tax deduction, or received any other type of tax concession before making these contributions.

non-dependant   There are two kinds of non-dependants. A dependant for superannuation purposes, but a non-dependant for tax purposes, may be eligible to receive death benefits from a super fund account when a fund member dies, but with benefits tax deducted. A non-dependant for both superannuation and tax purposes can only receive super benefits when paid to the deceased fund member's estate, and benefits tax will also be payable.

non-preserved benefits   If you have had a particular superannuation account since before 1999 you may also have some benefits known as non-preserved benefits. If you have non-preserved benefits, then the benefits will either be restricted non-preserved (which you can access when you terminate your employment), or unrestricted non-preserved benefits (which you can access at any time).

offsets   Also known as rebates, offsets can reduce the amount of income tax that you pay on your income by a deduction against your tax bill, rather than reducing your taxable income.

ordinary time earnings   In terms of the SG, this means ordinary hours of work, including over-award payments, shift or casual loading, performance bonuses or commissions, but not overtime.

pension   Regular payments from a superannuation account in the pension phase.

pension offset   A tax offset that is available on the taxable component of pension payments from superannuation accounts if you retire before the age of 60, or you receive a pension from an untaxed fund.

pension phase The period of time when a super account is paying a fund member regular amounts for the member's retirement.

permanent disability Insurance available in and outside super funds that pays you a lump sum, and sometimes regular payments over a number of years, if you suffer permanent disability that prevents you from working. In a super fund, permanent disability insurance is often combined with life insurance. Large super funds can often offer these types of insurance at cheaper rates than you could negotiate as an individual outside super.

platform *see* wrap administration.

preservation Superannuation rule that restricts access to your super benefits unless you satisfy a condition of release.

preservation age The minimum age that you can access your super benefits when you retire. Retirement generally involves signing a retirement declaration that you have ceased full-time employment and that you never intend to be gainfully employed for more than 10 hours per week. You must send the declaration to your super fund.

product disclosure statement (PDS) A legal document that explains the main features of a super fund, or other type of financial product.

real return Earnings from an investment after adjusting the investment return for the effects of inflation.

rent assistance If you rent a home in retirement and you are eligible for the Age Pension, you may receive an additional payment to help you cover your rent.

restricted non-preserved benefits Money in your super account that you cannot withdraw until you leave your job. Your super benefits may include this type of benefit if you were a super fund member before 1 July 1999.

retirement planning The process of creating a long-term strategy to build investments sufficient to maintain your chosen lifestyle for your retirement, taking into account your individual needs.

risk The chance that you take when you invest that you may lose part or all of your investment, or not generate as high a return as you hoped, or miss out on other investment opportunities because you put your money into this investment.

risk tolerance Your ability to cope with investment losses or volatile investment markets.

salary sacrifice   Deduction of concessional (before-tax) super contributions from your salary as part of a salary package, which reduces your taxable salary and the amount of income tax payable.

same sex couples and rights   In super and social security a same-sex couple is treated the same way as a heterosexual couple when applying for Age Pension entitlements, or when taking advantage of superannuation strategies related to couples.

self managed superannuation fund (DIY super fund)   A small super fund of no more than four members that is run by the members as trustees and is regulated by the ATO.

senior Australians tax offset (SATO)   If you are Age Pension age or older, you may be able to access this more generous tax-free threshold, which then reduces the tax payable on your income.

Six-Step Wealth Check   Trish's six steps are an easy-to-use process that can help you improve your life in retirement, helping you identify the lifestyle you want, how much money you will need to finance this lifestyle, and how you can reach this wealth target by the time you retire.

superannuation guarantee (SG)   Official description for your employer's compulsory superannuation contributions. The law currently requires your employer to pay the equivalent of 9 per cent of your wages or salary from your ordinary hours of work as super contributions when you earn more than $450 a month.

superannuation trustee   An individual or individuals or company that runs a super fund.

taxable component   The part of a superannuation benefit on which you will have to pay tax. You are likely to pay tax on this component if you receive a super benefit under the age of 60 or receive a benefit from an untaxed fund.

tax-deductible super contributions   Making concessional (before-tax) super contributions and claiming a tax deduction for those contributions in your individual income tax return, which reduces your taxable income and the amount of income tax payable.

tax-free component   A portion of a super benefit that is tax-free. Generally this component includes your non-concessional contributions, and certain pre–July 2007 benefits.

today's dollars   Today's dollars are what your future money would be worth if you spent it today.

transition-to-retirement pension (TRIP)   A superannuation pension that is available before you retire from the workforce. You can take out only up to 10 per cent of your account balance each year, and you must have reached your preservation age before starting a TRIP.

unrestricted non-preserved benefits   Money in your super account that is no longer subject to the preservation rules and can be withdrawn at any time.

untaxed fund   A super fund for which the government has not yet paid in the cash for the employer contributions (excluding SG contributions) that it has agreed to pay on behalf of public sector employees. That means that contributions tax has not yet been deducted from those unpaid super contributions and so the tax must be paid on withdrawal.

untaxed plan cap   A recipient of a benefit paid from an untaxed fund can receive concessional tax treatment of superannuation lump sum benefits up to this cap.

voluntary contributions   All super contributions other than compulsory employer (SG) contributions.

work bonus   Available for individuals receiving the Age Pension who remain in the workforce.

work test for over-65s   Once you turn 65, you must satisfy a work test to make super contributions: you must work for 40 hours in at least one 30-day period at some time during a financial year (1 July to following 30 June).

wrap administration   An administration product that operates as an information collection service. It gives investors access to a lot of managed funds, rather than a single investment product. A wrap service does all of the administration tasks that an investor has to do, such as records all transactions, including prices, brokerage, any GST payable, dividends paid and tax payable.

Index

Printed in Australia
05 Jan 2017
613832

9 781742 469713